Punchneedle
Creations

Punchneedle Creations

PAMELA GURNEY

SALLYMILNER
PUBLISHING

First published in 2006 by
Sally Milner Publishing Pty Ltd
734 Woodville Road
BINDA NSW 2583
AUSTRALIA

© Pamela Gurney 2006

Design: Anna Warren, Warren Ventures Pty Ltd
Editing: Anne Savage
Illustrations: Wendy Gorton
Photography: Tim Connolly

Printed in China

National Library of Australia Cataloguing-in-Publication data:
    Gurney, Pamela.
    Punchneedle creations.

    ISBN 9781863513593.

    ISBN 1 86351 359 0.

    1. Embroidery. 2. Punched work. I. Title. (Series :
Milner craft series).

    746.44

10 9 8 7 6 5 4 3 2 1

Acknowledgements

My family and close friends, with their unending help and enthusiasm, have allowed my passion to take flight by giving me time to concentrate on my beloved embroidery.

Heartfelt thanks go to my husband Peter for standing with me once again as we juggled with life, family and our business while I was preoccupied with designing, embroidering and writing.

Jenny and Kylie, my two dear, generous friends, have been a constant support with their humour, advice and help.

My very talented and creative artist friends, Ona and Syd, have spent many hours guiding me through the final stages of design for some of the projects.

I owe thanks to other punchneedle embroidery enthusiasts from all over the world who enjoy what I do and with whom I keep in touch through the marvellous world of the Internet. I also want to acknowledge everyone who has given me feedback and encouragement which has once again inspired me to put in the creative effort and months of work to write this book. Many of these people are customers, a number have become friends, many I have never personally met but their emails and messages are welcome and reassuring.

I have generously been given the pattern for Leesa's Bag by Leesa of Chandler's Cottage, and the doily design by Kath and Alan of The Stitchery.

The greatest wealth is doing what you love and there are many people who have helped me to continue with my love—my punchneedle embroidery.

To you all, thank you.

Profile

Pamela Gurney is a textile artist well-known throughout Australia and internationally for her beautiful punchneedle embroidery. Written from her home in the Australian bush outside Melbourne, this, her fourth book reflects the creative passion and versatility that Pamela brings to this gentle needle-art.

Over the years Pamela has explored the various ways of using punchneedle and that encourages others to create lovely conservative punch embroidery and also to 'step outside the square' to become creative embroiderers.

Pamela holds both a Diploma in Art/Design for Embroidery and 'Train the Trainer' qualifications. She has taught at hundreds of seminars, classes and workshops in Australia and New Zealand and is well-known around the world for her innovative and fresh approach to punchneedle embroidery. Pamela has built a business from her embroidery and 'Dancing Needle Designs' now sells punchneedle embroidery supplies both by mail order and e-commerce within Australia and internationally.

Pamela's work exemplifies how exciting and satisfying this embroidery technique can be.

Contents

THE PROJECTS

Introduction

I hope that this, my fourth book, will inspire beginners and more experienced embroiderers alike to enjoy punchneedle embroidery. I love this form of needle work, and it is exciting to know that so many people around the world are now also experimenting and finding enjoyment with punchneedle embroidery.

This book aims to encourage others to find pleasure from this gentle needle-art, to understand its traditions and techniques and to have satisfaction and relaxation from the needles that dance. About fourteen years ago I picked up a punchneedle for the first time. I truly loved the technique but at that time there was little information on punchneedle embroidery that excited and enthused me. Once I had learnt the basics and enjoyed 'traditional' punchneedle embroidery I then started to play and experiment with threads, fabrics, designs and colour. Life has been fulfilling since. My passion has increased over the years and has become my business. Peter, my husband, has joined me in my work and we travel widely showing, sharing, teaching and inspiring others to begin to dance freely with the art of punchneedle embroidery. The 'dance' with my punchneedles continues, and I sincerely hope that your needles dance forever.

PAMELA

1. Punchneedle Embroidery Explained: an overview

Punchneedle embroidery, worked with a special tool, a punchneedle, stands alone in its ability to create the most textural of all embroideries. Depending on the size of the punchneedle, this technique uses a vast array of threads and ribbons which can add life, colour, texture and richness to embroideries. Unlike traditional hand embroidery, punchneedle embroidery requires a design to be printed or traced onto the back of the fabric to be embroidered. With a threaded punchneedle, the embroiderer makes a small running stitch on the back of the fabric following the traced design. To form this running stitch, the fabric being used is held tightly in a special lip-lock hoop and the needle is 'punched' through to the front of the fabric where a loop of thread is formed. It is the loop on the front that outlines or fills in the embroidery.

With this technique amazing textures are created. The loops can be short, long, trimmed, fringed or shaped to give a wide range of textural effects to enhance a design.

To embroider this gentle needle-art, a design is traced onto the back of the fabric to be embroidered. The fabric is then placed into a special lip-lock hoop with the design uppermost where it is pulled very tight, thus opening up the weave. A beautiful little running stitch is worked on the back of the fabric, which in turn forms a loop on the front. The loop can be varied in length to create added depth. The whole process culminates in a unique, richly textured and highly dimensional embroidery. As I travel widely to share and teach the technique of punchneedle embroidery with thousands of people, it is apparent that the principle of punchneedle embroidery is not readily understood. A great number of people wonder why the loops of the embroidery stay in place. Punchneedle embroidery is worked from the back of the fabric and if the beginning tag of thread left on the back of the fabric is pulled, the stitching can be pulled out. That is the reality of it—that is the way it is. But understand that this happens from the back of the fabric. Turn the fabric over to the front and try to pull the loops from the fabric and you will find they do not readily pull out.

It is necessary to understand that with the technique of punchneedle embroidery it is the weave of the fabric that holds the loops in place. It is important for the punching process to have the fabric stretched extremely taut to open the weave of the fabric. When the fabric is stretched tight in the hoop, the weave is opened up. It is necessary for the weave to be open to allow the passage of the needle through the fibres.

Thus there is very little to hold the loop in place. Pull the tag of thread from the back while the fabric is in the hoop and yes, some loops can be pulled out. However, it is not so easy to pull out the loops from the front of the piece even when in the hoop. As well, the straight stitch made on the back of the fabric joins each loop and those stitches hold the loop in place. When the fabric is removed from the hoop the weave relaxes and closes around the loops and it is quite a different story—the stitches on the back, and the loops on the front, are equally secure and quite difficult to accidentally pull out.

There are a number of principles that need to be understood as to why the loops stay in place. Traditionally, punchneedle embroidery was designed to be worked with the stitches close together and thus the loops on the front of the embroidery are very close together. When worked like this it is extremely difficult for the loops to come undone. As well, because the punched stitches are close together the loops get caught up with each other, and the filaments of the spun and twisted threads become intermeshed. The loop when punched through the fabric also twists on itself a little and opens out, becoming bigger than the hole made for the passage of the needle. Further, if the completed embroidery is washed the threads and fabric shrink a little and some threads will matt as well. All these factors collectively explain why a completed piece of punchneedle embroidery cannot readily be pulled out.

Remember the importance of having the fabric very tight in the hoop so that the weave is stretched open, allowing the needle to easily penetrate the fabric without damaging the fibres. During the process of the embroidery there is very little holding the last stitches punched, and that is why when the tag is pulled some stitches can be undone from the back. A couple of backstitches at the beginning and end of the stitching can be worked for added security. See Stitch Glossary, Figure 7.

The principles above need to be understood for one to realise the difference between this method of embroidery and traditional hand embroidery, in which stitches are worked up and over the weave of the fabric to be held in place.

When punchneedle embroidery is worked in the normal manner, that is, with the punched loops very close together, a completed piece will wash and wash and have a very long life.

There are many other methods of stitching within the spectrum of punchneedle embroidery, aside from punching loops very close together, and some of these will not stand up to day-to-day use or washing. The pieces of embroidery which are embellished with surface stitches, such as reverse punchneedle embroidery (see Stitch Glossary), will need to be framed or have a smear of glue over the back of the stitching to hold the stitches in place.

2. Requirements

Punchneedles

There are many varieties of punchneedle available and they all work on the same basic principle—that being, a small running stitch resembling the stem stitch used in traditional hand embroidery is worked on the back of the fabric, which in turn forms a loop on the front of the fabric.

Generally a punchneedle has a handle and a metal needle tip. The handle may be made of brass, plastic or wood, with the needle tips made from stainless steel, surgical steel, brass or some other type of metal, depending on the age of the instrument. The handle and needle are hollow, allowing the passage of a thread through them. The needle tip has a bevelled (slanted) side and a straight side.

A variety of punchneedles in use today.

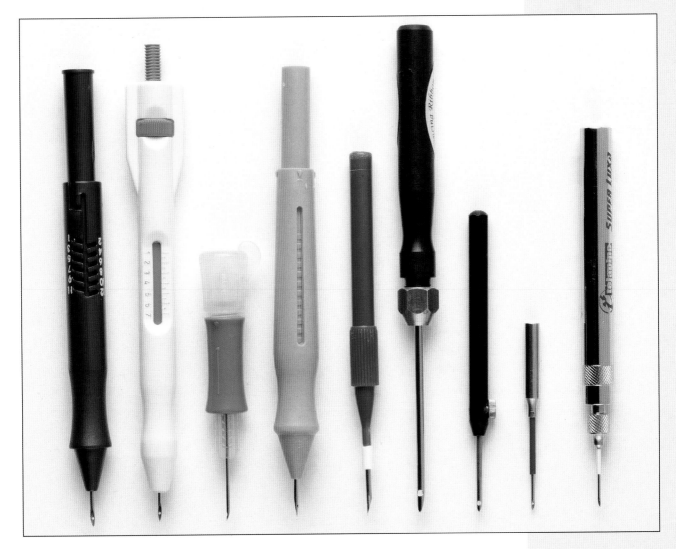

The eye of the punchneedle is a hole on the straight side of the needle. With some experimentation and adaptation, most types of punchneedles can be used to make interesting pieces of embroidery.

There are many brands of punchneedles currently available and whatever is used will be a personal choice dependent on the type of project that is to be undertaken

Regardless of the type of punchneedle used, the final result of a running stitch on the back forming a loop on the front will be achieved. The end effect can range from quite primitive to highly artistic depending on the tool and the execution of the stitch. The result achieved to some extent depends upon the implement's capabilities and some punchneedles will be able to do more or less than others.

Having punchneedles of different sizes is an advantage. Some punchneedles are so fine as to only allow very fine thread to be threaded through them. Others are larger, and some can take interchangeable needle tips which allow the use of fine threads, thicker thread, wool and ribbons.

The choice of punchneedle, be it very fine, small, medium or large, for a certain project will be dependent on the thread that is to be used and the type of fabric to be embroidered upon. If the chosen thread will flow freely through the punchneedle, then that is a good indication that the embroidery will be successful—so long as the fabric is suitable and is held very tight in an appropriate hoop.

It is best to initially work on a practice piece of fabric. Use this to check the type and thickness of thread that can be worked through the punchneedle and the type of fabric that the chosen punchneedle is most compatible with (see Chapter 2, Requirements: Threads, and Fabrics).

Depending on the punchneedle you have I hope that my ideas are a source of inspiration for you.

Pile Depth

Understanding about pile depth or the length of the loop made when embroidering will greatly assist in getting the best from the punchneedle that has been chosen. Each type of punchneedle has its own unique way of altering the length of the needle tip and thus the length of the loop formed on the front of the fabric—the pile depth. The needle tip can be punched through the fabric only as far as the handle of the punchneedle or to the end of a gauge placed on the needle. The gauge, or other methods such as springs or twisting mechanisms used on certain punchneedles, sets the depth to which the needle can be inserted into the fabric and gives evenness to the loops created.

Some punchneedles require a small piece of plastic tubing to be positioned over the needle tip to restrict how far the needle will go into the fabric. This can be seen on three of the punchneedles in the photograph on page 13. The plastic tubing alters the pile depth or loop size. For these punchneedles, one measures from the eye of the needle and then cuts the tubing to the length appropriate to give the pile depth required for a particular project. For punchneedles using plastic tubing, the plastic is either purchased with the punchneedle or alternatively can be made from the insulating plastic surrounding narrow-gauge electrical wire after removing the wire. If the plastic is initially too tight to slip onto the needle, soak it in warm water to soften it. It may be too loose, in which case pass a piece of thread through the tube to give the plastic a tighter fit when placed onto the needle.

The pile depth is measured from the eye of the needle to the end of the plastic tube being used as the gauge, or to the bottom of the handle in some types of punchneedles.

The length of the loop formed on the front of the fabric is half the measurement for the pile depth. A pile depth of 25 mm (1 in) will give a loop of 12 mm (½ in). Some of the length of the loop will be taken up by the thickness of the fabric. This needs to be considered if using a thick, fluffy woollen blanket fabric, for example.

Other punchneedles have built-in mechanisms which very easily alter the length of the needle. With some

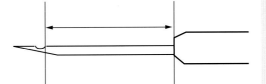

The distance between the vertical lines indicates the measurement for pile depth.

punchneedles, the needle holder within the casing of the handle is twisted up and down resulting in a longer or shorter needle tip. Yet another type of punchneedle has a spring and gauge which simply allows the needle holder in the handle casing to be pushed up and down and locked into different settings. This needle is particularly easy to use and to adjust the pile depth with the minimum of fuss and time.

Some needle tips have their length measured in millimetres, others by numbers and yet others by letters of the alphabet. For this book all needle tip measurements are given numerically, with the lowest number, No 1, being the shortest needle length. The guide on page 16 is applicable for conversion for various types of punchneedles to the projects in this book.

The guide on page 16 is applicable for conversion for various types of punchneedles to the projects in this book.

TIP

I have worked most of the designs in this book using the Ultra-Punchneedle (although Beautiful Brooches, Pretty Pink Blooms and Five Fabulous Daisies were worked with the Dancing Ribbon needle). It is important that you first experiment with your own punchneedles as your needle might work a little finer or larger than my needle. You may need to slightly alter the size of a pattern or use shorter or longer loops to accommodate your particular punchneedle.

| cm | 1 | 2 | 3 | 4 | 5 | 6 | 7 | 8 | 9 | 10 |
| in | | | 1 | | 2 | | 3 | | | 4 |

Conversion Chart

Setting	Needle length (mm)	Needle length (inches)
No 1	9–10 mm	⅜ inch
No 2	11–12 mm	approx. ½ inch
No 3	12–13 mm	½ inch
No 4	14 mm	⅝ inch
No 5	15 mm	a little over ⅝ inch
No 6	17 mm	approx. ¾ inch
No 7	18 mm	¾ inch
No 8	20 mm	a little over ¾ inch
No 9	21 mm	⅞ inch
No 10	23 mm	a little over ⅞ inch
No 11	25 mm	1 inch
No 12	26–27 mm	1 ⅛ inch

The conversion chart is approximate only, as needle tip lengths can vary. The projects in this book may be successfully worked with an allowance of needle tip length of 1–2 mm.

Very Short Loops

To make a very short loop, shorter than the shortest needle setting when using a gauge-controlled needle, cut a piece of plastic tubing and place it on the needle to shorten the length of the needle (see Stitch Glossary, Figure 15, sample b). If the tubing is cut too long it will result in a loop that is too short and which will not stay in the fabric. If this happens, shorten the length of the plastic by a millimetre or two and try again.

Plastic tubing, however, is optional. You can work at No 1 if there is no tubing available but sometimes the loops can look too long. They can be shortened by scratching the stitches gently on the back with a fingernail; this will shorten the loops which will give a finer appearance.

Long Loops

There are some projects which require the needle tip at a much longer length to produce long loops. This is achieved by removing the casing and spring from the large needle tip and handle, which leaves the full length of the needle tip exposed. Store the casing and spring away safely.

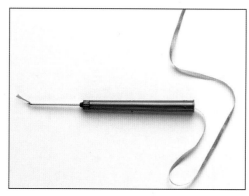

Outer casing removed from the needle and handle.

The length of the needle tip will now measure approximately 46 mm (1 ¼ in).

Ensure that with each 'punch' the needle tip is punched through the fabric up to the blue hilt of the needle. This will make a very long loop on the front of the embroidery which gives added dimension to certain embroideries.

Extra Long Loops

And yet again, there will be areas, such as in the design In a Coral Garden, where even longer loops are needed to add emphasis. To achieve the extra long loops, punch the needle tip with the casing removed to the hilt. Before withdrawing the needle, pull the threads from the eye of needle at the front of the work and hold in place while withdrawing the needle, thereby extending the loops in length.

The Dancing Ribbon Needle

This is an Australian-made punchneedle designed to embroider with 7–13 mm (approximately ¼–½ in) silk ribbon. The results achieved with the Dancing Ribbon needle are exquisite. The way one uses it is only a little different to the smaller types of punchneedle. In common with other punchneedle embroidery the design is marked on the back of the fabric and the project worked from there. After drawing the design and placing the fabric very taut in the hoop, the needle tip of the Dancing Ribbon needle is placed at the point of insertion and guided through

the fabric with a gentle twisting action. This allows the tip to delicately find its way between the fibres of the fabric without causing much damage. More precise instructions for its use appear with the project Beautiful Brooches.

The Dancing Ribbon needle can just as easily 'dance' with wools and thicker yarns threaded through it. This makes it the perfect tool for stunning ribbon embroidery and, on the other end of the scale, for making floor rugs.

Threaders

A threader with a paper or plastic tag

TIP

Without a fine wire threader, it is almost impossible to thread a punchneedle. Frequently threaders 'hide', fall on the floor or just get lost. If you have the type of threader with a small square of paper as a tag on the end, pierce the paper and tie some bright ribbon to it so that the threader is easy to find!

You will need to read the instructions with your punchneedle set to know how to thread your needle. As instructions sometimes get misplaced, the following is a general outline of how a punchneedle is threaded.

A threader, which is a specially adapted fine wire with a looped end, is required to thread a punchneedle. All punchneedles are threaded in a similar manner. Threaders have two loops, the larger of which the thread is initially passed through, and then the thread is gently pulled up, into the smaller loop which holds it in place while the thread is being pulled through the hollow of the needle. See Threading a Punchneedle for more specific instructions, and read the instructions which come with your punchneedle set.

Threaders are quite fragile and easily broken, therefore they require gentle handling.

Threading a Punchneedle

Threading a punchneedle is a two-part process, first threading the bore of the needle and then threading the eye of the needle.

Step 1 The threader is first inserted from the sharp end of the needle tip, up through the hollow bore of the needle and handle until the looped end of the threader protrudes from the handle.

Step 2 Pass the thread through the big loop and pull it into the small twisted loop at the end of the threader. The twisted loop holds the thread securely while it is pulled down the bore of the needle.

CARE AND SAFETY

The precise machining of punchneedles means they need to be carefully looked after. The tips need to be protected to prevent them from becoming damaged or burred by being dropped or stabbed into harsh objects. Some punchneedles have a spring-loaded action which enables the needle tip to be retracted and housed safely. Others come with plastic sheaths in which the needle tip is placed when not in use.

It is important that punchneedles be kept out of reach of toddlers, and that children use them only under close supervision. These are long sharp implements which can cause a nasty scratch or prick. Work safely.

Step 3 Pull the threader by the attached paper tag all the way back through the handle and needle until the threader and thread are clear of the needle tip. Unthread the thread from the threader. The eye of the needle is yet to be threaded.

Step 4 Insert the fine twisted looped end of the threader from the straight side (eye side) of the needle through the eye of the needle.

Step 5 Insert the thread again through the big loop of the threader and pull the thread up into the small loop to hold it in place, draw the thread back through the eye of the needle.

Step 6 Remove the thread from the threader and carefully put the threader away and the threaded punchneedle to one side until ready to commence embroidering.

Backwards or Reverse Threading

There will be times when the punchneedle becomes unthreaded while the embroidery is in progress, leaving an end of thread attached to the back of the embroidery. It can often be a short length or the very last of a particular colour, and if it was cut off in anticipation of re-threading, it will be too short and almost impossible to thread.

TIP

It is important to remember that threading the punchneedle is a two-part process. Often one reason that a punchneedle does not work properly is that the thread has only been passed through the handle and bore of the needle and not through the eye of the needle.

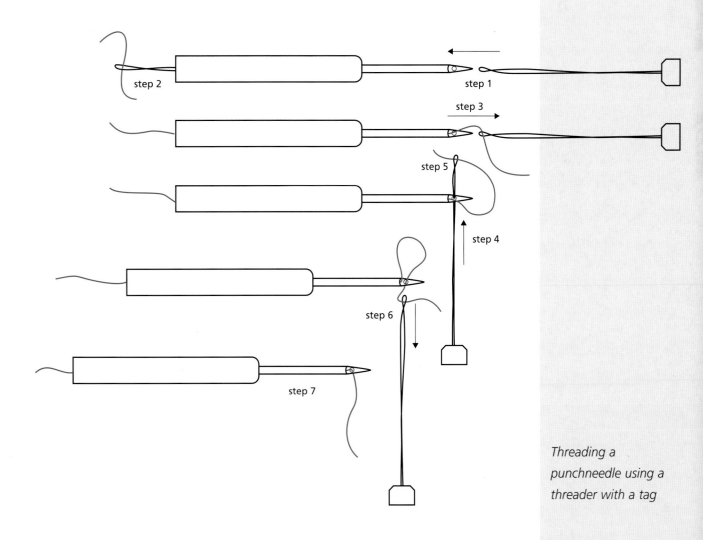

Threading a punchneedle using a threader with a tag

This 'precious' piece of thread can be pulled back into the needle in reverse. Where a threader with a paper tag is the only type available, the paper tag needs to be removed.

Thread the threader from the angle side through the eye. Thread the thread into the small loop of the threader and pull it through the eye of the needle. Leave the thread in the threader and push the untagged end of the threader from the tip end of the needle, through the hollow of the needle and out through the handle. Tighten the thread, remove the threader and position the needle tip on the fabric in preparation to commence further stitching.

Threads and Ribbons

The wondrous thing about punchneedle embroidery is the variety of effects created by using the many different thicknesses, textures and colours of the threads which are readily available in craft shops. The colours, types, thickness, shine and tex-tures of the myriad threads to be found are exciting. All of these factors add the 'shimmer' phenomenon to an embroidery.

A vast range of threads and ribbons which can be threaded through the eye of a punchneedle and will flow smoothly through it can be used for punchneedle embroidery. Any thread can be used if it passes this test. Very often, when there is trouble with the thread flowing, all that is needed to fix the problem is simply to choose either a larger needle or a finer thread. Equally, a sign that the thread may be too thick for your needle is when the loops being embroidered do not stay in place in the fabric you are punching through.

The thread can sometimes be too fine for the punchneedle; this will generally be a single strand of thread that seems to 'fall' through the needle in a rush, leaving a loop where the needle penetrates the fabric. If this happens, change to a needle with a smaller bore size or, occasionally and gently, pull back the thread at the handle end of the punchneedle as you work. Increasing the tension of the fabric in the hoop by pushing up from underneath with your fingers helps as well. Often it is a case of experimenting and trying different combinations of threads, needles and fabric to discover what works best and, if there are any limitations, what they are.

From one strand of thread up to six strands, 2 mm to 4 mm silk ribbon, some tapestry wools and crewel wool, crochet cotton, candlewick thread, machine embroidery threads and various exotic threads can be worked through an appropriate sized punchneedle. The thread thickness that can be used is determined by the bore (inside diameter) of the punchneedle—the only requirement is that the thread must flow through the eye of the needle smoothly and evenly.

The Dancing Ribbon needle adds further astonishing effects to punchneedle embroidery as it has the capability of using 7–13 mm (¼–½ in) silk ribbon and thicker wools, yarns and exotic threads.

For the projects in this book many types of threads have been used for the effects and variety that can be achieved. Use different types of punchneedles for

TIP

It is possible to thread some large punchneedles such as the Dancing Ribbon Needle in one movement. Push the threader through the eye of the needle, bend the tip of the threader slightly and guide it into the bore of the needle. Push the threader all the way through the bore and handle until it shows. Pass the thread through the twisted loop of the threader and then pull the threader back through the bore and the needle in one motion. (See Threading under Dancing Ribbon Needle.)

different projects and understand that some threads and ribbons work well in some needles and not in others. You will need to experiment with your own punchneedles and learn their limitations and capabilities. This is part of the enjoyment and magic of punchneedle embroidery!

The threads used in these projects have been chosen because they are generally readily available. You can substitute other threads if a particular one is not easy to find—always remembering the rule, of course, that if a thread type does not flow through your punchneedle, change it.

Acrylic Yarn

Acrylic yarn, referred to as 'traditional punchneedle embroidery acrylic yarn', is used widely for traditional punchneedle embroidery. These yarns, although sold under a number of different brand names, are all very similar.

Acrylic yarn has many really good and valuable qualities. It flows freely through the punchneedle and stays easily in the fabric, owing to the fact that the filaments which constitute the yarn clutch in on themselves. It works up quickly and gives a wonderful full effect, very similar to the effect achieved by

Materials used in punchneedle embroidery.

using crewel wool. Acrylic yarn is available on a large spool from which it may be directly worked. This is a great timesaver as it is not necessary to re-thread the needle so often. Worked with stitches very close together, embroidery with acrylic yarn becomes durable and washable. Again this is due to the filaments on the fibres intermingling with each other. When washed the fibres matt together, making it almost impossible to undo any of the stitching. It can also be brushed and sculpted.

These yarns work up quite differently to a cotton or silk thread when embroidered with a punchneedle. The main difference between acrylic yarn and embroidery cotton, using the same sized punchneedle and the same needle length, is that the size of the formed loops with the acrylic yarn is shorter than with embroidery cotton (see the photograph in Chapter 3 Techniques, under How Much Thread?). This is because the acrylic yarn is made up of small filaments which make it embroider a little like fine wool—the fibres within the yarn cling to each other and also to the fabric when the punchneedle penetrates it, thus not so much thread goes through the fabric, resulting in a shorter loop. Cotton or silk threads, being smoother, flow more easily through the needle and work more effortlessly through the fabric. When working acrylic yarn in designs specifically developed for other threads it may be helpful to increase the needle length to give a longer loop.

The acrylic yarn equates in bulk to approximately six strands of Madeira, DMC or other embroidery cottons. One thickness of acrylic yarn works well through the medium punchneedle, as do six strands of embroidery cotton. Use the large punchneedle for two thicknesses of acrylic yarn.

While vibrant and interesting colours are available in acrylic yarns, the colour range is limited when compared to embroidery cotton. This makes for some difficulties in directly matching colours from the cotton and silk ranges to acrylic yarn for specific designs. Where possible, acrylic yarn colours have been recommended to replace Madeira or DMC cotton threads in certain projects. It is important to know that if traditional punchneedle embroidery acrylic yarn is not available, then any 6-stranded embroidery cotton will be a suitable substitute, or a fine wool such as crewel embroidery wool. Any design that is worked with a brand or type of thread not specifically recommended can give unsatisfactory results.

Blending colours with acrylic yarns is difficult as there is no gentle gradation of colours in these ranges.

A finished piece of acrylic yarn embroidery may be ironed over the back with a warm iron. The heat assists in matting up the fibres of the yarn, thereby adding another explanation for why punchneedle embroidery is durable and wearable.

Loose filaments of the yarn can rest on the finished embroidery or stick onto the fabric. A handy way to remove these filaments is by using sticky-tape—pat the sticky side of the tape gently over the embroidery to pick them up.

When using acrylic yarn, if the hoop is

not large enough and needs to be moved around, it seemingly does not damage the yarn when the hoop is repositioned and tightened over already punched loops. When the hoop is removed the loops are flattened but can be easily lifted by using a fingernail or by giving the area a shot of steam from a steam iron.

Embroidery Cotton (Embroidery Floss)

There are many brands of embroidery cotton, or floss. It is a thread made up from six separate strands which can be pulled apart, and then from one strand through to six strands can be used effectively for punchneedle embroidery. Different brands of embroidery cotton have different characteristics.

Tapestry and Crewel Wool

There are many types of wool that can be successfully used through an appropriately sized punchneedle. Tapestry wool, and crewel wool specifically used for wool embroidery, are good choices, but there can be marked differences between the thicknesses of various brands. It is best to thread the needle with the chosen wool to check that it flows easily through the eye of the needle. Testing for the flow is done by pulling the wool from the needle end and then from where it exits the handle to feel if the wool moves easily within the bore of the needle and through the eye. Some wool seems to not flow easily but it can actually be the 'burrs' on the fibres that restrict it. Stretch the fabric tightly in the hoop and embroider a few rows of stitches to check that it will actually

work. Tapestry wool is worked through a large punchneedle whereas crewel wool will be used through a medium sized punchneedle.

The embroidery for the Floral Bouquet in Wool uses both tapestry and crewel wool, and has been worked on doctor's flannel, a finer woven wool than woollen blanketing.

Thicker wools can be embroidered through the Dancing Ribbon needle.

Rajmahal Art Silk

This is a viscose thread with similar properties to some rayon threads. It is made up of six strands which can be separated; from two strands through to all six can be used, depending on the size of the punchneedle. Rajmahal thread has a brilliant lustre and comes in a wide range of vibrant, beautiful colours which strikingly enhance any embroidery.

For the punchneedle embroiderer, Rajmahal offers one minor challenge. It is shiny and slippery and the starting and finishing threads often slip through to the front of the fabric. There are a couple of ways around this. Firstly, when the punchneedle is threaded, tie a small knot in the end of the thread. This at least holds some ends in place. Secondly, smearing a little washable craft glue on the trimmed ends as each section is finished is worth considering. To do this, squeeze a very tiny amount of glue onto a small piece of paper. Dip a pin into the glue and smear a small amount of it onto the end of the thread. When dry this will hold the first and last stitches neatly in place.

It is worthwhile to learn about the

TIP

I have touched on only a few types of threads, those which I have used in this book. There is an abundance of threads. Head off to your nearest craft store or use the Internet to find out what is available. With punchneedle embroidery there is a choice of needle sizes, so many threads can be used for the embroidery so long as the thread will easily flow through the needle. If the chosen thread has difficulty flowing through the punchneedle or it flows through too quickly and without control, chances are it is the thread that is the problem, not the punchneedle. Simply change the thread or change the size of the punchneedle. See also Punchneedles, above.

properties of Rajmahal art silks and to use them for the spectacular results which can be achieved in a piece of embroidery.

Silk Ribbons

The ribbons of interest to a punchneedle embroiderer will be either 2 mm or 4 mm silk ribbons for medium to large punchneedles, or 7–13 mm (¼–½ in) ribbons worked through the Dancing Ribbon needle, specifically designed for them (read more on this in the project Beautiful Brooches). The ribbon needs to flow easily through the chosen punchneedle. Ribbons can be in plain colours or hand-dyed, in any of the many brands available from specialist embroidery and craft shops. Silk ribbons are usually much softer than the polyester ribbons so widely available; the thickness of polyester ribbons means they will not be easily threaded through the eye of the punchneedle. It is therefore important to use a very soft ribbon and to test the threading and its flow through the chosen punchneedle.

Gold and Glittery Threads

Gold threads and glitters enhance or give 'zing' to a piece of embroidery. When used with a normal needle in traditional embroidery, gold threads shred easily as the outer gold filaments strip away from the central strand they are wrapped around, and only small lengths are used, to prevent wear and tear and breaking as the gold thread is constantly passed through the fabric. This problem is not so apparent with punchneedle embroidery

as the gold thread is only being punched through the fabric once for each loop—this means that long lengths of gold thread can be used with only few, if any breakages. There are many brands and thickness of gold and glitter threads—experiment with readily available threads to find a favourite.

To name just a few—Madeira Metallic, Article No 9805, colours 5017, 5012 and my favourite, 5014 (used sparingly in Jewelled Wings 1) are wonderful to use. DMC Mouline Metallisé is made up of very fine strands which can easily be separated. You can add to this Rajmahal machine/hand sew polyester metallic threads, Au Papillon (Butterfly) thread, to liven up any piece of embroidery.

Designs and Ideas

One of the first things to consider is to have a definite design or idea before starting punchneedle embroidery. Draw inspirations for patterns and designs from fabrics, wrapping paper, magazines, cards, dinnerware and children's books. There are complete iron-on transfer books; punchneedle embroidery books with both designs and instructions, as well as patterns and kits specifically designed for punchneedle embroidery from many embroidery designers. There is a difference between being inspired by something which you have seen, and copying someone else's design. Be mindful of the issue of copyright and take this into consideration. For your own peace of mind and to protect artists, take time to understand copyright issues. The projects for this book have been designed to give enjoyment and provide a challenge for the embroiderer. Some of the projects have been expressly chosen to include a lesson within them. There are important hints and tips scattered in and about all of the projects. Read through the project instructions and hints before starting to embroider a particular design. This will provide an overall understanding of the techniques involved and if necessary you can refer back to the relevant technique elsewhere in the book to clarify an issue before you begin the piece of embroidery.

Fabrics

A tightly woven fabric is required for punchneedle embroidery. It is important to know and understand that it is primarily the weave of the fabric that holds the embroidered loops in place (see Chapter 1). Punchneedles may damage some fabrics and care needs to be taken when choosing a fabric on which to embroider.

There is a huge range of fabrics to choose from. A fabric which contains a proportion of polyester seems to give the best results. Other fabrics can be used, but be aware that there are many qualities and types. Some experimenting is needed and it is a good idea to try various fabrics to find the types that work best with a punchneedle. A perfect fabric for punchneedle embroidery is American weaver's cloth, which is composed of polyester and cotton, or an Australian fabric with poly/viscose/flax blend.

Experiment with other fabric such as silks, moiré, taffetas, changing the needle size where necessary and knowing that if the needle damages the fabric an iron-on interfacing (see page 27) can be used.

When shopping for a fabric look for a relatively tightly woven fabric. Check that there is very little stretch to it. Calico (muslin) and some cotton patchwork fabrics, although woven, stretch a great deal when pulled tightly in the lip-lock hoop.

Check this characteristic before proceeding with a particular fabric because the direction of the stretch, depending on whether it is along the warp or weft, can distort the shape of a design. The warp is the lengthwise fibres following the selvedge, whereas the weft is made up of threads crossing from side to side. If a design of a bear, for instance, is traced onto fabric with a lot of stretch, then pulled tight in the hoop and embroidered, the finished bear might be long and skinny, or short and fat, depending on which way of the stretch the design was traced and embroidered onto the fabric.

It is only necessary to pre-wash fabric which may have a tendency to shrink if the finished item is likely to be washed, such as a piece of clothing. The sizing present in unwashed fabrics appears not to damage the punchneedles.

Testing a sample of fabric before starting on a project can reduce the risk of failure and frustration. Place a sample of the chosen fabric in a hoop and work a few rows of stitching with the punchneedle and thread that you intend using. Undo the trial stitching and have a good look at the fabric to see if it is damaged. If you can coax the warp and weft back into place with a fingernail where the punchneedle has made an opening, and the surrounding fibres have not been damaged, then the fabric is generally suitable to use. If the fabric is visibly damaged, an iron-on woven interfacing applied to the back of it will strengthen it, and usually the embroidery can proceed without further concern.

The stretchy fabrics used for sweatshirts need to have an iron-on woven interfacing bonded onto the back before commencing the embroidery, remembering that it is the weave of the fabric that holds the loop in place. The interfacing needs to be bigger than the hoop used so that the two layers of fabric are stretched together. At the completion of the embroidery the interfacing can be peeled back carefully and cut away to the edge of the embroidery. An alternative to working directly onto this type of fabric is to use the appliqué method, which eliminates the need to work on the actual stretch fabric. (See Appliqué in Chapter 3.)

Woollen fabrics have a tendency to stretch considerably when tightened in the hoop and it is also more difficult to actually get the fabric very tight, which is certainly a drawback when using it. It will be necessary at times when embroidering on wool to add more tightness to the fabric either by working over a bowl (see Hoop Techniques in Chapter 3) or by pushing the fabric up from behind, using quite a bit of pressure with the fingers. If the fabric is not tight it is difficult with some woollen fabric to get the needle tip through the fibres and the loops to stay in place. Uneven loops occur when the fabric is not tight enough in the hoop.

The bulkiness of thick woollen blanketing makes it difficult to get this fabric sufficiently taut in the hoop to work satisfactorily. However, as there are so many types of blanketing it is wise to have a practice with any chosen blanketing. If the blanket fabric holds the loops, there is no reason not to work directly onto it. If it is too open in weave, the loops will not stay in place. The appliqué method is also an ideal alternative to working directly onto wool blanketing or terry towelling and stretchy knit fabrics. An iron-on interfacing can be used on the back of woollen blanketing, but be aware that the heat required for bonding may damage the wool fibres. An option is to stitch a woven fabric onto the back. Use short running stitches (with a sewing needle and thread) and stitch in a grid with the rows about 6 mm (¼ in) apart. This grid can be embroidered over with a punchneedle, and when the embroidery is finished the outer stitches are removed and the backing fabric is cut carefully away to the punched outline.

Always be aware of the thickness of the fabric and the need to have it taut in the hoop. Wool flannel, also known as doctor's flannel, is an option to wool blanketing as it is not as thick. Both tapestry and crewel wool through the appropriate punchneedle can be used on it. See the project Floral Bouquet in Wool.

There are so many beautiful fabrics to choose from and often it is only through experimenting that you will find which fabrics work more successfully than others.

Hoops

Many suitable hoops are available and the choice will be the one that best suits a project. An ideal type is the plastic lip-lock hoop. This hoop has an inner ring with a lip, and an outer ring with a nut for tightening. When the lip on the inner hoop is positioned up and over the outer ring and the nut is done up tightly, the fabric is held secure and very taut (drum-tight) which is the optimum for punchneedle embroidery. (See How to Get Fabric Tight in the Hoop in Chapter 3, Techniques.)

The 'Perfect' Hoop Nut

The Perfect hoop nut can be tightened with fingers, a coin, a small screwdriver or the small metal ruler which is also ideal for measuring needle tip lengths. Once the Perfect hoop nut doesn't easily turn further, refrain from over-tightening, as this can lead to stripping the thread of the screw.

Also, often when tightening the hoop with the existing hoop nut, the oils from the fingers can mark the fabric, as the fingers and thumb roll against the fabric. This problem is minimised when using the Perfect hoop nut.

Pony Bead

The screw on some lip-lock hoops occasionally has insufficient thread to allow the hoop to be adequately tightened. This problem can sometimes be overcome by removing the hoop nut

and placing a plastic 'pony bead' on the screw (see photo). Replace the hoop nut and tighten as much as is possible against the pony bead.

Iron-on Woven Interfacing

Iron-on woven interfacing has a special coating on the back which melts when heat is applied and bonds onto the main fabric.

Where a fabric which is too fine and fragile in nature for the size of punchneedle you intend to use has been chosen, you will have to consider using interfacing. Not all fabrics will require it. Test your chosen fabric—if the punchneedle damages the fibres, then consider using a woven iron-on interfacing or choose another fabric.

Use a woven interfacing as opposed to the knitted varieties available for dress-making. Before ironing the interfacing into place, check that there are no bits of fluff or hair caught between the two layers, as these can show up noticeably through some fabrics and spoil the look of a finished piece of work. It is necessary to bond the

This Australian hand-crafted brass nut is used to replace the existing hoop nut on a lip-lock hoop. The existing nut is often difficult to grasp to tighten sufficiently, especially for those who have problems with their hands or sore arthritic fingers.

interfacing very well to the fabric. When the fabric with the interfacing bonded to it is pulled very tightly in a hoop the interfacing, if not adhered strongly, can come apart from the fabric. When this happens any loops worked can be lost between the two layers.

Other Tools
Light-box

A light-box is a box with a glass top under which is a light. When a design and fabric are placed over the lit box, the outline of the design readily shows through the fabric for ease of tracing. However, if you do not have access to a light-box then a well-lit window works equally well. Hold or tape the traced pattern with the fabric over it, onto a window. With the light shining through it is easy to see the outline which needs to be traced. Use a sharp lead pencil, water-erasable pen or a heat-transfer pen.

Design Transfer Tools

Tools for transferring designs to fabric include the heat-transfer pen, dressmaker's carbon (both dark and white) and the water-erasable pen. Their methods of use are discussed in Chapter 3, Techniques.

Scissors

Small, sharp, pointed embroidery scissors are essential for trimming threads, sculpting and shaping. With sharp, pointy scissors, threads on the back can be trimmed close to the fabric. Blunt, rough scissors can very easily pull out worked loops.

Ruler

A small ruler is often required for measuring needle lengths and the small pieces of plastic tubing used for altering the length of the needle tip on punchneedles that do not have a gauge or settings for this purpose. Stainless steel rulers (see photo of equipment earlier in this chapter) with the markings going to the very end are the perfect tool, as they are normally gradated in both inches and millimetres. A stainless steel ruler is also ideal for tightening the Perfect hoop nut.

Other rulers have the measured markings beginning a few millimetres in from the end. If a small plastic ruler is the only one available, cut the end off with an old pair of scissors so that the first measurements are at the very end of the ruler. This makes measuring the needle length so much easier.

Craft Glue

There are many types of fabric glue available. Choose acid-free glue and look for qualities such as it being clear, soft and pliable when it dries and that is washable, such as You Can Wash It craft glue. It is used to seal the cut edges of appliqué work and can be lightly smeared onto the back of a completed piece of embroidery to give added security to the formed loops to prevent them being accidentally pulled out. It can also be used on the beginning and end of threads to prevent them slipping through to the front of an embroidery.

Pressure-sensitive Craft Glue

This glue is applied to the back of an appliqué design and left to dry until it is tacky. The appliqué can then be pressed onto a garment where it remains secure until removed. The tackiness lasts for many applications before the glue needs to be replenished. Using this type of Off'N'On glue gives great versatility to an appliqué design when it is not necessary to have it adhered permanently.

Crochet Hook

Refrain from cutting any threads on the front of the work, as threads change colour when cut and leave dark marks which show up dramatically on the finished work—this is why a crochet hook is a valuable punchneedle embroiderer's tool.

A fine steel crochet hook is useful to pull any long loops or ends that show up on the front of the embroidery through to the back. Be extremely careful when using the hook, as it is easy to get it caught in the thread and to pull out too many loops. When retracting the crochet hook do so with a gentle, twisting action.

Tweezers

Tweezers are invaluable and most useful when working reverse punchneedle embroidery, where the beginning and ending threads need to be pulled to the back of the fabric.

Pellon

Pellon is a soft, thin wadding sometimes used in quilting. It is ideal to use with a completed piece of punchneedle embroidery, particularly where reverse punchneedle embroidery has been incorporated. With reverse punchneedle embroidery the punched loops are formed on the back of the embroidery. During framing when the fabric is stretched by the framer, the loops bulge out through the fabric and look unsightly in the finished and framed piece. Place pellon under the fabric before stretching it and the loops nestle into the softness and 'disappear'.

3. Techniques

Preparing to Embroider

Assemble the fabric very tightly in the hoop (see Hoop Techniques, further on in this chapter). Position the hoop nut at 12 o'clock and facing to the right if you are right-handed (to the left for left-handed embroiderers). The nut will then be mostly out of the way when embroidering which will prevent the working thread from getting caught around it.

Straighten the design in the hoop as it can become distorted during the tight stretching process.

Thread the punchneedle as described in Chapter 2. Check the flow of the thread by pulling it gently to and fro through the needle. If it is too tight or too loose, either change the needle size or change the thread.

Look at the needle tip. There is a bevelled edge, that is, the edge cut on a slant, and a straight edge with the eye.

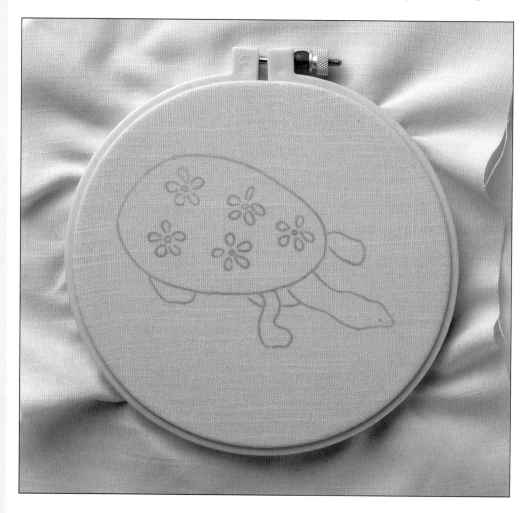

Fabric tight and the weave of the fabric straight in the hoop. Note—the inner ring positioned up and over the outer ring of the hoop.

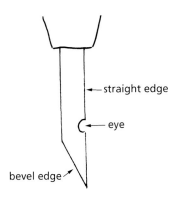

An enlarged view of a punchneedle tip showing the bevelled (slanted) edge and the eye of the needle.

Direction of Work

For the best results when embroidering with a punchneedle, stitch forward towards the body and constantly turn the hoop when stitching so that the needle is always travelling forward. A right-handed person will have the bevelled edge of the needle facing to the left while stitching and the eye of the needle to the right. For left-handed people turn the bevel to the right and the eye to the left.

The way to work with the punchneedle is personal and may differ from that described. Work in whatever manner is most comfortable, so long as the formed loops look good, give adequate coverage on the front of the fabric, and are even in length.

It is best to sit up at a table. To begin, hold the hoop with the nut positioned at 12 o'clock and rest one side of the hoop on the tabletop at the position of 3 o'clock, at the same time holding the other side of the hoop high enough above the table so as not to punch into the tabletop and thereby damage the tip of the needle. Reverse this if left-handed.

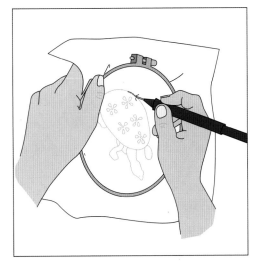

Getting Ready to Make the First Stitch

Normally when working punchneedle embroidery, the stitches are worked from the back of the fabric to the front, so the side of the fabric with the design traced onto it needs to be uppermost in the hoop. It is far easier to stitch on the flat, tight, upper face of the fabric in the hoop than to work into the concavity of the hoop.

Hold the punchneedle like a pen. Rest the side of your hand and your little finger on the stretched fabric. It is best that the hoop is not held underneath with the little finger of your stitching hand. Your hand needs to be free to move unrestricted, to 'dance' over the fabric.

Hold the punchneedle at a little less than right angles to the fabric (that is, slightly off the vertical, as in the photograph) or hold the punchneedle in whatever manner is comfortable.

There is no set place to start stitching. If an outline is to be worked, start at any point on that line or wherever on the design that the instructions suggest that you start.

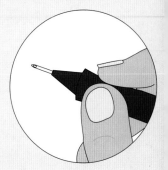

This is the ideal way to hold the hoop when stitching. It illustrates the angle at which the punchneedle is held and the position of the bevelled edge of the needle tip.

31

Work safely. Be sure to keep your fingers away from the underside of the fabric where they might get pricked.

How to Make the Stitch

There is no knotting, tying or oversewing to begin or end the stitching in punchneedle embroidery. A couple of backstitches to start and finish can be made for extra security, however this is not necessary and is optional (see Stitch Glossary, Figure 7). Work two stitches backwards, and then stitch forward immediately on top of these. This assists in holding the beginning and ending stitches in place.

With the needle on the setting appropriate for the pattern, punch through the fabric as far as the needle can be punched. Every stitch is punched to the full depth of either the plastic on the needle tip or, if the needle length (pile depth) is set by a gauge, to the hilt of the needle. Each stitch punched fully to this depth gives uniformity to the length of the loops formed on the front of the fabric.

A tag of thread will be left on the back of the fabric at the point of entry of the needle. This needs to be only about 6 mm (¼ in) long, depending on the thread being used. The ends of some fine or slippery threads can have a tendency to find their way to the front of the fabric, however. If that is the case, leave a longer tag and trim later.

Withdraw the punchneedle a little and turn it in your fingers until you can see the start of the bevel. Position the bevel to face to the left if right-handed or to the right if left-handed. Withdraw the needle until the tip barely clears the surface of the fabric. Skim the needle along the surface for a very short distance and punch it into the fabric again. Listen to the dragging sound this makes for the first dozen or so stitches until the action becomes natural. The motion for working becomes a lift to the surface-slide-punch, lift to the surface-slide-punch action. Avoid lifting the needle tip clear away from the fabric as this can pull the loops you have just punched out from the front of the fabric.

An indicator of how far apart the straight stitches made on the back of the fabric need to be is approximately the width of the needle being used. It takes only a short time before becoming aware of how long the stitches need to be and how closely you need to work the rows.

Turn the embroidery over to check the progress. If stitches are close enough together on the back they will make an unbroken row of loops on the front. If there are gaps in the line of the loops, this indicates that the stitches on the back need to be a bit closer together. When a second row of stitches is made close to the first row, the loops of that row will fill up any small spaces of the previous row on the front of the fabric. The loops at this stage can seem to be sparse; in particular, if two rows have been worked, there can be a definite space between the rows which initially for a beginner can be a concern. As further rows are embroidered the punched loops begin to fill over the fabric; if this isn't happening the stitching needs to be closer on the back to give a more filled-in look to the loops on the front.

Be sure that the thread is flowing freely through the needle and is not knotted or caught around anything.

The preferred method of stitching is to be working forward. This means that the hoop is turned constantly. To turn the embroidery leave the needle in the fabric, hold its position and pivot the hoop gently on the needle, which then turns the design on the fabric. In most instances when the needle is held in position turning the hoop as the embroidery progresses sets the needle tip facing in the correct direction.

Whenever possible, it is important to have the needle angled away from the row of stitches just worked. A right-handed embroiderer will work with the straight edge of the needle on the left side of the previous row of stitches (left-handed embroiderers will work opposite to this).

During the stitching process avoid punching into the previous row of stitches—if this happens, already formed loops can be punched and pushed longer than desired.

If a right-handed embroiderer works on the right side of the previous row with the needle angled towards the left, it is easy for the loops of the previous row to be punched through, and also to be pushed longer than the desired length. In this situation the front loops can look scruffy, and time and patience will be needed to tidy them up. When this occurs and longer loops form on the front, gently pull the loop down to the desired length with a fine crochet hook from the back, while the embroidery is tight in the hoop.

There will be some instances when it is necessary to work from the 'wrong' side of a previous row. Work slowly and carefully in these situations and, if necessary, tidy up the front of the embroidery as described above.

It is quite acceptable to change from one area of colour on the design to another of the same colour without cutting the thread. Hold the thread in place at the point of exit, pull the punchneedle along the thread, start in the new area and, when a few stitches have been punched, trim the looped thread between the areas. Keep the back of your work free from loops and long ends as these can easily get caught and pull out previously worked loops.

Check the loop spacing on the front of the work. The distance between the stitches is short and the distance between the rows is barely a needle width. When the finished piece is held up to the light, ideally there will be no gaps or unworked areas of fabric to be seen. If there are gaps, simply fill in with a few more stitches. A happy medium needs to be reached. If the stitching and rows are worked too closely the piece will curl up when removed from the hoop, if not close enough, the coverage on the front will be patchy.

At the beginning of an embroidery, when only one or two rows of loops have been made and are looked at from the front of a piece, it is so easy to say, 'Oh, it looks terrible', and to wonder if you are working correctly. The more loops that are made and the more rows that are worked the better the overall effect becomes.

TIP

An important technique to give the best appearance to a finished piece of embroidery such as Jewelled Wings or Leesa's Bag is to practise getting unbroken outside edges by working the loops very, very close together.

Keep checking the front of the work to see that the loops are all the same height. If there are loops that are sitting higher, very gently and from the back of the work, push the fine crochet hook through the embroidery at the place of the higher loop, hook the loop and gently twist the crochet hook out of the fabric, thereby reducing the length of the loop until it is flush with the others. Not having the fabric sufficiently tight in the hoop can cause uneven lengths of loops.

When a length of thread is almost finished, allow the thread to flow all the way through the needle. Sometimes the ends of the thread finish up on the front of the work and need to be carefully pulled through to the back with the crochet hook.

The fabric needs to be very tight in the hoop at all times. While embroidering, regularly tighten the fabric and re-tighten the hoop nut as necessary. Read the section on Hoop Techniques for further ideas. If the fabric becomes only slightly slack, gentle pressure can be applied with fingers to push up from under the hoop or down from the top of the fabric with the thumb to create more tension.

Cutting Threads

To cut the thread upon completion of a section of stitching, hold it in place with your index finger at the point of exit. The last loops made may be pulled out if the thread is not held firmly. Slide the needle some way along the thread, then punch the needle into the fabric for safekeeping

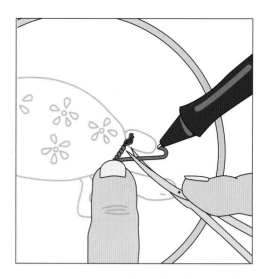

and to prevent it rolling. Cut the thread leaving a short tag.

If there are any thread tags or long loops on the front of the embroidery, pull them to the back of the fabric before trimming them. A crochet hook is helpful for this. Any long threads which appear on the front of the embroidery can be cut, but be aware that some threads change colour dramatically when cut and can show up noticeably as a very different colour or looking like a dirty mark. This is a technique that can be used to great advantage where a deeper shade of a colour will add effect to a design.

Finishing Off

On the completion of a project check the appearance of the work from the front before removing it from the hoop. The front may require tidying up—any long loops and end tags need to be pulled to the back—or more loops may need to be embroidered to fill in sparse areas of embroidery. Tidy and trim long threads on the back.

How Much Thread?

When embroidering with punchneedles, where the length of loop can be either uniform or varied, it is often difficult to determine how much thread will be required.

Also, when a pattern states, for example, to use 2-ply acrylic yarn, then how much cotton thread will be needed if it is substituted?

One way to deal with this quandary is to work up a sample piece. Draw a number of 1 cm (⅜ in) squares onto a piece of fabric which is then stretched tightly in a hoop, and into each square embroider with a variety of threads and yarns. Measure off a metre or a yard of the chosen thread prior to starting by placing a pin or a piece of tape as the marker. Fill in the area and if all of the thread is not used, subtract the remaining length from the measured length. Alternatively, if more thread is required, measure another length and add this to the first measured amount. Make a note beside the sample of the length of thread used, as these samples will be a valuable reference. Alternatively, work the samples, pull out all the stitching and measure the length of thread used.

Estimate approximately how many of the sample squares will fit into an area to be embroidered and use that as a gauge as to the amount of thread required.

What the three samples show is that punchneedle embroidery actually uses a considerable amount of thread and that various threads use different quantities.

It also demonstrates that the loops of yarns which have noticeable filaments

attached to them which clutch onto the fabric, such as acrylic yarn and wools, have a shorter length of loop than the cotton thread which is smoother. It is quite noticeable that sample c, although worked similarly to samples a and b, has a longer loop length.

Working with Silk Ribbon

Embroidering with silk ribbon is slightly different to embroidering with threads and yarns. These instructions refer to working 2–4 mm wide silk ribbons with a larger size of punchneedle. Instructions for working 7 mm and 13 mm silk ribbons with the Dancing Ribbon Needle are included with the project Beautiful Brooches, the first of the three projects in this book that uses the Dancing Ribbon needle.

A large needle tip threaded with 2–4 mm silk ribbon might damage the fibres of the fabric when punched through the fabric. Thus, the motion of using the punchneedle is to gently twist the needle tip carefully through the weave of the fabric and to push the needle tip down as far as it can go. Avoid the usual punch-punch-punch motion when using silk ribbons. Use a motion of gently twisting through the weave and then pushing the needle tip.

Usually with punchneedle embroidery there is no knotting or tying to commence the stitching, but silk ribbon is slippery, and can very quickly and frustratingly become unthreaded from the punchneedle. Also, the beginning tag of the silk ribbon frequently finds its way through to the front of the fabric. Therefore, when the needle is threaded, a small knot can be tied on the end of the ribbon protruding from the needle tip. The knot will keep the needle threaded and will stop the beginning tag from working its way through to the front of the fabric.

A length of ribbon sufficient to tie a knot in the end tag can be left when you have finished working, but this can waste expensive ribbon. A knot at the beginning is sufficient, as it at least prevents some of the ends from escaping through to the front.

A smear of glue on the end of the ribbon at the completion of each area will help to keep the end tags in place.

If an end of ribbon does find its way through to the front of the fabric, use a small crochet hook to carefully grasp it and pull it through again to the back.

When embroidering with silk ribbon, any long loops already created are held out of the way of other loops being punched through the fabric. This is to prevent the punchneedle piercing them, which makes them look tatty. It also prevents the long loops becoming intermingled or embroidered together, which in turn prevents the petals from opening fully. While holding long loops out of the way on the front of the fabric, embroider slowly, working safely and gently to prevent stabbing your fingers.

When each area or flower is completed, check on the front of the embroidery that the long loops are not caught in other loops. If they are, gently release them with your fingers. See the 4 mm silk project, the Superb Silks on Satin cushion.

The Dancing Ribbon needle, a special punchneedle for use with wide ribbons, very easily and beautifully embroiders 7 mm (¼ in) and 13 mm (½ in) silk ribbon. See the instructions for embroidering with the Dancing Ribbon needle with the project Beautiful Brooches, and the projects Pretty Pink Blooms and Five Fabulous Daisies.

Dealing with Fabric of Different Sizes

The fabric needs to be large enough to fit into the hoop with sufficient allowance to be pulled on when tightening the fabric.

As it is necessary to frequently turn the work over to check the progress of the embroidery, working with a large piece of fabric can be a nuisance—it often gets caught on things, knocking things onto the floor and just simply getting in the way. If it is necessary to work with a large piece of fabric, roll up the edges and secure with safety pins to make working easier and safer.

If you have a special piece of fabric which is too small to fit into the hoop, stitch calico borders onto it to make it large enough. (See A Note on Old Fabrics.)

Transferring the Design

There are many methods for transferring a design onto fabric, including the use of a light-box, heat-transfer pens and pencils, water-erasable pens or dressmaker's carbon. There will be instances where one method prevails over another.

Heat-transfer Pen

An easy way to get a design onto fabric is with a heat-transfer pen. The design is traced from the original source, or from a black and white photocopy, onto tracing or computer paper. The traced image is turned over and placed into position onto the back of the fabric, and heated with an iron set at the appropriate heat for the fabric being used. The hotter the iron, the darker the imprint will be. If a light imprint is required, apply less heat or alternatively, prior to transferring the image remove some of the darkness of the traced lines by ironing the tracing onto a clean sheet of paper a few times to take away some of the ink.

Refrain from sliding the iron over the back of the paper as the tracing may smudge if the paper moves at all.

Diagrams to be transferred are drawn facing the same way as the front of the completed design. When these are traced onto fabric using the iron-on transfer pen, the tracing will show in the reverse. When the traced diagram is embroidered from the back with punchneedle embroidery the finished piece, which is viewed from the front, will be facing the same way as the original diagram.

Store the tracing when finished, as it can be used quite a number of times before the transferred design becomes too light. Make sure the cap of the iron-on pen is replaced when not in use.

Iron-on Transfer Pencils

Iron-on transfer pencils are an easy way of transferring a design onto fabric. They are used in the same way as a heat-transfer pen. A minor problem with the iron-on transfer pencil is the difficulty of achieving a truly fine line. Sharpen the pencil frequently and wipe the tip before using, as granules of colour can fall on to your work.

Dressmaker's Carbon

White or coloured dressmaker's carbon is useful where there is a need to transfer a design onto black or a dark fabric, as the design outlines can readily be seen. The marks can be removed with a damp cloth.

Water-erasable Pen

Water-erasable pen lines are ideal for marking an image onto fabric where a permanent image is not desired. A design traced onto the front of the fabric with this pen in preparation for reverse punchneedle embroidery (see Stitch Glossary, Figure 3) can easily be removed with a damp cloth. Some types of pens are available with a fine tip at one end and a thick tip at the other. The punchneedle can have a slight problem punching easily through the ink left on the fabric of some brands of these erasable markers.

Transferring a Design onto Dark Fabric

If a dark fabric is chosen it can be difficult to get a design traced onto it but there are various ways that this can be done. A white marker pen is useful, or iron a white iron-on woven interfacing onto the back of the fabric and then use a design traced with the heat transfer pen to get the required image onto the white interfacing.

As well, dressmaker's carbon is ideal—put the fabric onto a hard surface, place the carbon face down. Place the design to trace over that and then with a stylus or the ball of a crochet hook go over the design with sufficient pressure so that the carbon imprint is made onto the fabric.

With the last method there is the problem that the image can easily be erased with the embroidery hand constantly moving over it.

Marking the Straight Grain of the Fabric

An extremely important consideration when transferring a design onto fabric is that it is placed on the straight of the fabric. Marking the straight grain allows you to position a design accurately.

This technique is particularly useful when a precise geometric design is being worked, such as preparing to embroider a miniature carpet, as for the project Jewelled Wings 2. Marking is done using a crochet hook, with the fabric stretched very tightly in the hoop. Place the back (the ball) of the hook onto the fabric between two rows of weave. Press down and drag the ball firmly between the two rows. This separates the fibres slightly and leaves a mark which is easy to see and to work along. This line may look slightly crooked when stretched in the hoop but it straightens when the fabric is removed from the hoop.

Hoop Techniques

With punchneedle embroidery it is very important to have the fabric stretched as tightly as possible in a hoop. When the

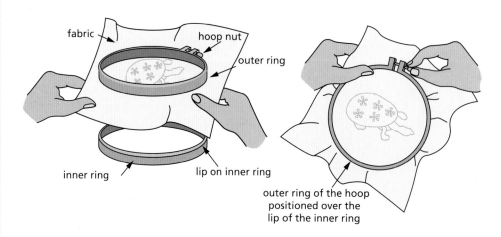

fabric
hoop nut
outer ring
inner ring
lip on inner ring

outer ring of the hoop positioned over the lip of the inner ring

fabric is drum-tight, the weave of the fabric is opened up and this allows the punchneedle to find its way easily between the fibres.

If the fabric is not tight in the hoop, the loops worked in punchneedle embroidery will be uneven. The punchneedle technique is also more enjoyable when the fabric is tight in the hoop. The needle can find its way easily between the fibres, the loops stay in place, progress is made and everything works beautifully. Working with fabric which is not pulled taut means that it is more difficult to punch the needle through the fabric. The needle has trouble finding its way between the fibres of the fabric, the fabric can become damaged and the loops do not readily stay in place. As well, a great deal of stress is placed on the wrist and forearm, which can prove painful over time.

At times the outline of a design can become distorted when the fabric is stretched in the hoop. Pull the fabric in the hoop to make the design as near to the original tracing as is possible before beginning the tightening process.

Be aware that it is possible to have the hoop nut done up very tightly and the fabric still not tight in the hoop. It is a step-by-step process to tighten the fabric.

Turn the assembled hoop and fabric so that the fabric is resting on the table top. Put your fingers inside the hoop and your thumbs over the fabric on the outside. Work around the hoop, pulling the fabric tight, up and over the centre of the hoop. At every quarter pull the fabric and turn the hoop. Repeat the process. Tighten the hoop nut after each complete round.

Repeat the whole process three or four times until the fabric is drum-tight and the hoop nut cannot be tightened further. As a final measure, pick the hoop up, turn it over and pull tightly on the corners of the fabric all the way around.

The lip-lock hoop which is nearly always sold with a punchneedle set generally has a small hoop nut for tightening. This is quite hard to get hold of and for people with sore, weak or arthritic fingers is often difficult to tighten. A brass nut, called the Perfect hoop nut, which is much easier to manage, is available to replace the existing nut (see Chapter 2 Requirements).

Unfortunately, due to the tightness required of the fabric, an impression of the hoop can be left on the fabric which can be visible when the finished embroidery is framed or, for example, made into a cushion. It is possible to remove such marks by steaming with an iron or pressing with a Rajah cloth (a chemically treated ironing cloth). A pressing cloth moistened with white vinegar and water can also be useful. Always remove any dirty marks before pressing, as the heat from an iron can set them permanently. Occasionally, however, it is impossible to remove the impressed mark, which is especially disappointing when a great deal of work has gone into a project (see Using a Doughnut).

Further Help with Getting the Fabric Tight

If great difficulty is being experienced in getting the fabric tight enough, one option is to tighten it as much as possible and then place the assembled hoop over a pudding bowl or a wooden bowl which fits inside the hoop. The embroidery is worked over the bowl. As the embroidery is being pushed down over the bowl and the pressure from the bowl pushes up, added tension is given to the fabric. Take care that the needle tip is not accidentally punched into the sides of the bowl which may damage the tip.

Using a Doughnut

There is one small drawback to using the special lip-lock hoop with the fabric pulled drum-tight. The hoop sometimes leaves a circular mark imprinted on the fabric which is particularly difficult to remove. To prevent such marks developing consider the use of a 'doughnut'.

A doughnut is a square of calico or similar fabric the same size as the fabric being embroidered, with the centre cut out to reveal the design. This is placed over the front of the embroidery fabric before the two pieces are assembled together in the hoop. A second doughnut can be placed at the back of the fabric to further assist in softening the impression of the hoop. Work the embroidery

A doughnut protects the fabric from dirty marks and hoop impressions.

through the hole in the doughnut.

Also, if the design being worked on is larger than the hoop size, the embroidery will need to be worked in sections and when the hoop is moved it will be placed over some of the embroidery, as in the Delightful Doily project. It is normally quite safe to do so as long as good quality threads have been used. When the hoop is removed the stitching underneath it will be flattened. These flat areas can be raised up by scratching on the loops with a fingernail or by holding a steam iron over the affected area in the same way that one raises the plush of velvet.

If there is a concern about the loops being squashed because the hoop is not big enough and needs to be moved during embroidery, a doughnut will protect already embroidered areas. It will need to be repositioned whenever the hoop is moved.

Dirty Marks

The use of a doughnut will also protect the fabric from the dirty marks resulting from the natural oils in your skin, especially when the hoop nut is being constantly tightened and the thumb rubs upon the fabric. One needs to be aware that these dirty marks occur far too easily, are cumulative and are often not noticed until the piece is nearly completed or being prepared for framing. These marks can usually be removed by gently rubbing the area with a clean cloth moistened with water with the addition of a little white vinegar or a very small amount of soap. Gently rub the offending mark. Move the cloth around to a clean spot, moisten it with clean water and gently rub the area to dry it.

Cord Making

Cords add a delightful touch to completed embroideries such as the Superb Silks on Satin cushion and Leesa's Bag. They can be made in two different ways, by the finger method or with a cord-making tool.

Cords made by the finger method stay twisted when let go and do not readily unravel and are finer in appearance.

A cord maker, also known as a Spinster (see photo in Chapter 2 Requirements) speeds up the process a great deal. This tool looks something like a small hand-held drill used for woodwork, but where the drill piece fits there is a small hook. Beautiful, long cords can be made with a cord maker, which has full instructions included with this natty tool when it is purchased.

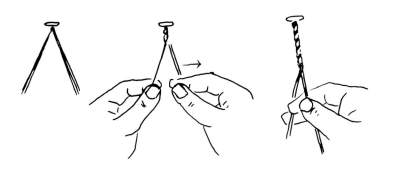

Making a hand-made cord.

Hand-made Cord

To make a cord of a given length by this method you need to start with threads that are about 3 times longer.

Cut four or six lengths of the chosen thread/yarn. Knot them together at one end. Divide the threads into two equal amounts.

Hold the knotted end in the left hand or secure it to a firm surface with a pin.

Take the threads on the right side between the right-hand index finger and the thumb and twist them tightly to the right.

Pass the right-hand threads over the left ones; now take the second group of threads between the index finger and thumb of the right hand and twist these to the right.

Reverse the way of holding the thread if left-handed.

Repeat this process until you have a length of cord sufficient for your purpose. Tie a knot at the end.

Appliqué

There are many places where appliquéing a design to a background is beneficial. A design can be embroidered onto a piece of fabric with a punchneedle, cut out and then attached elsewhere. The Tortoise Flower Power design on the baby capsule cover has been made like this. The appliqué method is ideal if you want to embellish a stretch-knit sweatshirt instead of embroidering directly onto it. Appliqués can give extra dimension to the look of a finished piece of work.

Embroider the design. Remove the fabric from the hoop and stretch it in all directions to straighten the embroidery. Glue over the outside edge of the completed design and about 6 mm (¼ in) onto the fabric all around it. Be sure to impregnate the fabric with glue as some fabrics can fray when cut if there is not sufficient glue to prevent this. Allow to dry. Cut the embroidered design away from the fabric with a small, sharp pair of scissors. Take care not to cut any loops; however, if you do, simply put a little glue on a pin tip and press this onto the cut loop, pushing the loop back into place.

To make it less obvious that the design has been appliquéd, wherever possible work the design on a background fabric similar in colour to the outside row of stitching. For example, work on black fabric if the outside edge of the embroidery is worked in black. Where a black outline stitch is used on a pale fabric, the pale cut edge will be more obvious and can detract from the finished item.

You can also paint the outside edge to match before cutting and then touch up the areas which haven't taken the paint when it was cut, but note that sometimes the glue used on the back will prevent the fabric taking on the paint. Methods of applying colour can include watercolour pencils, a matching felt-tip pen or fabric paints.

In some situations, to counteract the problem of the colour of the base fabric showing, it may be simpler to work the outside edge at a longer loop length.

The embroidered cut-out can be permanently attached with You Can Wash It craft glue. Alternatively, pressure-sensitive Off'N'On glue can be used if the cut-out is not required to be attached permanently. Prior to this glue being used, it is necessary to seal all over the back of the completed design with the washable craft glue. With the use of pressure-sensitive glue you can wear your beautiful creations on a range of different clothing or accessories as they can easily be moved. For more detail see Craft Glue and Pressure-sensitive Glue in Chapter 2 Requirements.

The Use of Glue

Traditionally, punchneedle embroidery was designed to be worked with the loops very close together and with short loops close to the fabric. When worked in this manner, the embroidery will hold in place very securely and can generally be safely washed (see also under Appliqué above). When appliquéd on knitted sweatshirt fabric, punchneedle embroidery will far outlast the garment itself, even after much washing.

Many decorative, surface stitches can be seen in the Stitch Glossary. These stitches generally rely for their effect on being worked on the front of the embroidery, mostly with only one row of decorative stitching standing alone. One row of punchneedle embroidery cannot be expected to stay in place through wear and tear and washing. This was never the intention for the technique of decorative punchneedle embroidery and this is when a gentle smear of glue to help hold the stitches permanently in place is necessary. Where these decorative stitches are used on a piece of embroidery for framing, it is best that they do not have glue on them. A framed

piece is special and needs to be framed as conservatively as possible to give many years of enjoyment. As the framed piece will not be handled or need washing, the stitches will not be at risk of being accidentally pulled out.

There will, however, be times when surface stitches are used on pieces of punchneedle embroidery used for interior home decoration, for example cushions, bedspreads or table runners. In these instances it is best that where a single row of decorative surface stitching is embroidered that a light smear of good quality craft glue is applied to the loops on the back. The decorative stitches when lightly glued become more stable, and are unlikely to be accidentally pulled out and will wash very well.

Repairing Holes in Fabric

Small holes can be made on the fabric being worked upon by the needle tip cutting a fibre, where dense punching has been worked in one area or a mistake has been made and unpicked a number of times, thereby weakening the base fabric.

◆ The damaged area can be 'darned'. Stitch in replacement warp and weft fibres with an ordinary sewing needle. The newly made fibres can be carefully punched into.

◆ Remove the fabric from the hoop. Take a small piece of iron-on woven interfacing and, with the tip of a heated iron, press the piece in place.

◆ If iron-on woven interfacing is not available, simply lightly glue a piece of woven fabric into place. Leave to

TIP

Often when a punch-embroidered appliqué has been cut out, points such as a hen's beak, a fish's fin or tail are not as crisp as they might be. This is probably because the outside row of stitching has not been worked closely enough together. An easy remedy is to put a small quantity of glue between the thumb and index finger, take the point and gently squeeze it, leaving a fine residue of glue which sharpens the point.

dry before doing any further gentle punching.

- Hold a piece of woven fabric over the damaged area and gently punch some loops through this. Trim the fabric when the area has been repaired.
- With a sewing needle threaded with a matching colour stitch some loops the same height. Lay a pin across the hole on the back to give the loops something to anchor onto and work over it. Glue over the back of the loops and before the glue is completely dry, remove the pin.

Creating a Coloured Background

Many people do not have the appropriate equipment or confidence to paint their own fabrics. The use of an iron-on Rainbow transfer paper is an easy way to add colour to a background. This paper

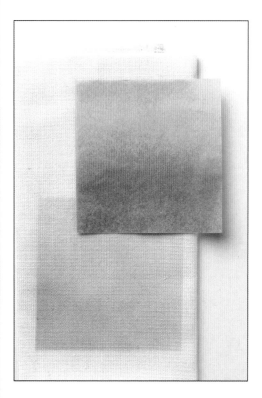

has the colours of the rainbow impregnated into it. It is ironed, coloured side down, onto to the right side of the fabric to transfer the colour. This is by far the easiest method to colour fabric. The colours transfer to the fabric in delicate hues and give added life to some of the plainer cream and white fabrics often used for embroidery. This paper has been used to colour the fabric background for the first project, the Lovely Lavender card.

Another idea is to tear the paper into small pieces and scatter them onto the fabric, especially in and around the outside edges of a floral design, to add interest and shadow effects. A similar effect can be seen in the Bear in a Garden design.

The depth of colour varies with the type of fabric being used, but is enhanced on polyester-based fabrics. Also, the hotter the iron, the brighter and darker the colours. Due care needs to be taken to prevent scorching of the fabric.

The colour from the transfer paper is wash-fast and seems to be permanent. However, it is worthwhile to do a wash test on a selected fabric before going to great efforts on the embroidery. Some fabrics might not hold the colours as well as others.

Caring for Your Embroidery

Washing

Punchneedle embroidery, when worked in the manner it was originally designed, with loops short and close together, as in the projects Jewelled Wings and Tortoise

Flower Power, washes very well. This is particularly so if it is embroidered with punchneedle embroidery acrylic yarn and embroidery cotton. Oftentimes the embroidery far outlasts the garment it is attached to. Due care is required when washing, to ensure the finished piece doesn't come into contact with Velcro or sharp fasteners which may catch on the loops.

Embroideries worked with larger loops and other threads are best washed gently by hand, just as one washes other sensitive garments or fabrics, as some types of threads do not have the same qualities as cotton or yarn and therefore other factors need to be considered when washing.

Pieces incorporating reverse punchneedle embroidery (see Stitch Glossary) which is not densely punched, and where the stitching is not close together, require careful washing as the stitching may begin to come undone. Where a piece with reverse punchneedle embroidery on it is to be washed, sparingly smear the loops on the back with You Can Wash It craft glue which remains soft and pliable when laundered. When the glue dries it will hold the loops on the back of the piece in place, and is added insurance against any damage or pulled stitches.

Pressing

It is best not to iron over a completed piece of punchneedle embroidery. If the need to do so arises, place the embroidery face down on to a thick, fluffy towel and press into the pile of the towel. Alternatively, use a steam iron in the same manner as working with velvet, holding the iron above the piece and allowing the steam to raise up the pile.

It may be necessary to steam press the fabric around the actual embroidery to remove the mark made by the hoop. This is a good reason for getting into the habit of using a doughnut (see Using a Doughnut on page 40).

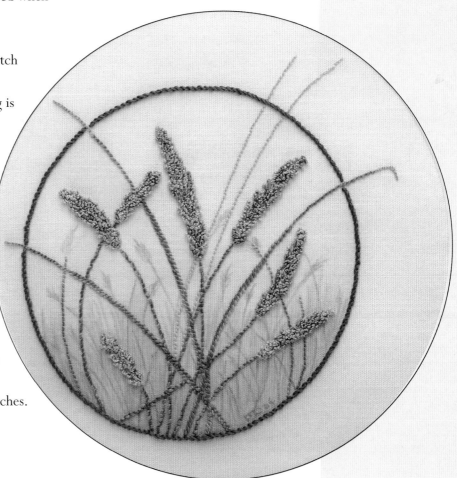

4. Stitch Glossary

Punchneedle embroidery is a fascinating needle-art. It is so versatile as there are many ways that the one basic, simple stitch of this technique can be employed to create an almost never-ending series of effects rich in texture. A huge range of threads, yarns and ribbons can be used if the ones chosen flow readily and easily through the eye of the punchneedle.

The embroidery samples in this book illustrate some of the diverse stitch variations which can be made when embroidering with a punchneedle.

Traditional Punchneedle Embroidery

Traditional punchneedle embroidery, the basis of all punchneedle embroidery (commonly referred to as 'normal punchneedle embroidery'), is small, straight running stitches punched from the back of the fabric which form loops on the front. The design being used is traced onto the back of the fabric and the embroidery is worked from the back of the fabric. There is no knotting or tying of the starting and finishing thread ends in this technique.

A variety of textures can then be created by altering between short loops and long loops. The long loops can be

cut, trimmed, fringed, sculpted or merely left as large, full loops. The result is always spectacular.

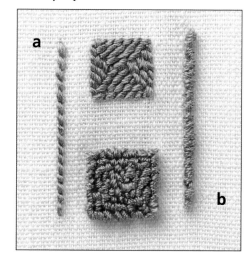

Figure 1 *Traditional punchneedle embroidery worked with six strands of embroidery cotton in the medium punchneedle.*

Sample a The top square and the line of stitching on the left show normal punchneedle embroidery viewed from the back, where a small running stitch is created. The tag which is normally left on the back has been cut very short for the purposes of photography (it is usually left a bit longer).

Sample b The bottom square and the line of stitches on the right show the loops which are formed on the front.

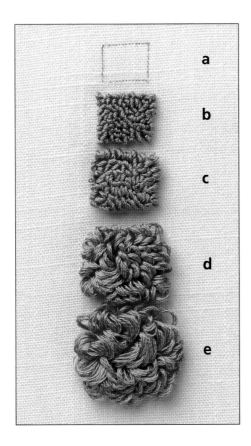

Figure 2 *Traditional punchneedle embroidery worked in six strands of embroidery cotton in the medium punchneedle with varying length of loops—**b** at No 1, **c** at No 4, **d** at No 8 and **e** at No 12.*

The box drawn on the fabric (**a**) is the same size as the box that all the samples have been worked in. By increasing the length of the needle and then punching through the fabric to the handle or plastic gauge of the needle with each stitch, larger loops are created on the front of the fabric. The larger the loops on the front of the fabric, the more area is occupied by the stitches. Sample e shows how much more fabric area outside the drawn square is taken up by the embroidery when the loops made on the front are longer.

Reverse Punchneedle Embroidery

See Figure 3, sample a.

Traditional punchneedle is a small running stitch on one side of the fabric which produces a loop on the other side—this is the basis of punchneedle embroidery. When this running stitch is worked from the front of the fabric an interesting surface stitch is created which alters the whole concept of punchneedle embroidery. This is known as 'reverse punchneedle embroidery', and by using it a host of different surface stitches can be executed, which offers a new and exciting entrée into the wonderland of punchneedle embroidery.

Ideally, for complete control and to achieve perfect stitches it is best if reverse punchneedle embroidery is done with the design facing uppermost in the hoop. It can be embroidered from within the concavity of the hoop but it is not so easy. Trace a very fine and light line with either a well-sharpened lead pencil or a water-erasable pen. The finished embroidery normally covers over the traced line.

To get the perfect reverse stitch it is essential to have the fabric as taut as possible in the hoop and to practice. How to achieve this is explained in Hoop Techniques in Chapter 3.

The beginning and ending threads of reverse punchneedle embroidery need to be pulled through to the back of the piece being embroidered.

To do this, simply punch the needle into the front of the fabric. Then turn the hoop over with the needle still in situ, and either with fingers or a fine pair of pointy tweezers, pull the thread emerging from the fabric through to the back. This is the starting tag of the thread. To shorten this tag, take the thread where it enters the handle of the punchneedle and withdraw it until only a short tag remains. This is all a bit of a juggling act, but with practice it becomes second nature. Complete the area to be stitched.

To get the finishing end through to the back, leave the punchneedle in the fabric. Turn the hoop over and with fingers or tweezers take the thread emerging from the eye of the needle and pull it to a sufficient length to cut it. Take care, as at this time, if the thread is pulled from the base of the fabric some stitches can be pulled out. Cut the thread. Withdraw the punchneedle from the fabric, leaving the end tag on the back. As the punchneedle is withdrawn, hold the last stitch made in place.

After removing the needle there may be a small entry hole left in the fabric. From the back use the nail of the index finger to scratch the fibres of the weave to close the hole around the thread.

Reverse punchneedle embroidery leaves loops on the back of the fabric. When a completed piece of embroidery worked with a lot of reverse stitching is stretched for framing the loops can cause a bulge which looks a little unsightly. This can be easily overcome by placing wadding or pellon under the embroidery on completion. The loops nestle into the soft padding, which prevents a bulge appearing when the piece is mounted for framing.

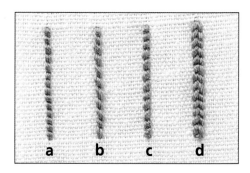

Figure 3 *The different appearances or finishes which can be achieved with reverse punchneedle embroidery. Six strands of embroidery cotton have been used in the medium punchneedle for these samples which are embroidered on the front of the fabric.*

Sample a Shows how the standard reverse stitch looks when worked with the bevelled edge of the needle directly forward. The running stitch appears to be straight.

Sample b Shows the beautiful effect given to the running stitch when the bevelled edge of the needle is facing to the left for right-handed embroiderers (or facing to the right for left-handed embroiderers) and stitching forward. This looks like the most perfect stem stitch made with traditional hand embroidery.

Sample c The bevelled edge is facing the left; however, the stitch is worked backwards. The difference in the look of the stitch is subtle but it is more raised. Thicker threads give it a bolder finish.

Sample d A row of stitching is worked forward, with a second row worked backwards close to it on the left, giving a lovely chain/rope effect to the reverse punchneedle embroidery.

Counting Stitches

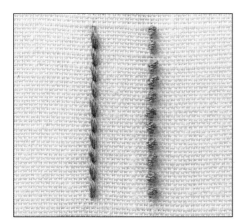

Figure 4 *Ten stitches, as counted on the back of the work, produce 11 loops on the front.*

For the designs in this book, the number of stitches which need to be embroidered are given in the instructions. This refers to the straight running stitch formed either on the front or back of the embroidery.

Punch the needle into the fabric and withdraw it. This leaves a loop on the other side. This is *not* counted as a stitch. Punch the needle into the fabric again, and count the first straight stitch linking the two loops created on the front as stitch number one. Continue punching and counting the stitches until the required number has been worked. Figure 4 is an exaggerated example of this for ease of viewing. There are 10 counted stitches which will produce 11 loops.

The number of stitches suggested in the instructions for each project are a guide only, as everyone works differently. It might be that more or less stitches are needed for the required area of embroidery.

Working in a Circle

When working in a circle has been mastered the technique of punchneedle embroidery enters a different realm. It opens up a vast new breadth to the form of traditional punchneedle embroidery.

Read the section on Direction of Work in Chapter 3, Techniques, where it mentions that when stitching with the punchneedle, the needle travels directly forward. The hoop is turned constantly so that this is achieved. To work a circle it is a constant movement of punching a few stitches, turning the hoop, punching and turning, punching and turning until the circle is completed.

Look at Figure 5, sample 1a, to see the first step of working in a circle.

Sample 1a From the back the needle is punched into the fabric. The beginning tag of thread remains on the back. This can be trimmed later. Take the first stitch very close to the tag and up to 12 o'clock. With the bevel of the needle facing to the left, punch one stitch to the left of the first stitch. Punch one stitch directly forward from the second stitch and very close to the tag. Leave the needle in the fabric. Turn the hoop clockwise a little so that you continue to work toward yourself. Punch in another one or two stitches and again turn the hoop. Continue in this manner until 20 stitches have been worked.

Hold the thread in place, withdraw the needle and cut the thread. When the embroidery is turned over a small round cluster of stitches resembling a

Figure 5 Circles transformed into stunning flowers: showing the appearance from the back on the left, and the appearance from the front on the right, as the circle is enlarged. These samples have been embroidered with six strands of embroidery cotton in the medium punchneedle.

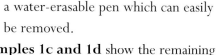
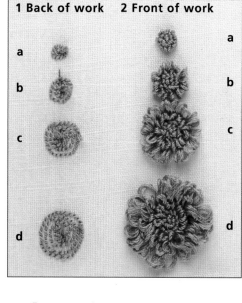

1 Back of work   2 Front of work

a

b

c

d

3 A flower embroidered with acrylic yarn

4 A ribbon flower with a centre of 6-stranded embroidery cotton

flower can be seen (sample 2a). If there is a hole in the middle of the flower and it looks like a doughnut, punch some more stitches to fill in the space. Practice making more circle-flowers, working very close to the beginning tag of the first stitch until perfect flowers are formed.

Sample 1b The horizontal mark on the fabric indicates where to begin and end the next rounds of stitches. Although it is marked in pen for clarity in this photo, refrain from using pen on your embroidery. For simple guide marks it is wiser to use a water-erasable pen which can easily be removed.

Samples 1c and 1d show the remaining rows which make up the flower. There is a slight space left between each row. This space allows the loops of each row to blossom out instead of being scrunched tightly together.

Sample 2b The needle tip has been altered to No 4. When changing the length of the needle tip it can be left in the fabric and altered in situ. Alternatively, hold the last worked stitch in place and completely withdraw the needle from the fabric, change the length, and tighten the excess thread by pulling it back from where it emerges from the handle. Stitch all the way around the circle. It is not necessary to count these stitches—work from the marked line and finish the round on the marked line.

Sample 2c The needle tip is set at No 8 for this round.

Sample 2d The needle tip is set at No 12. Stitch all the way around.

Sample 3 This has been worked in exactly the same way as sample 2, but with 2-ply punchneedle embroidery acrylic yarn. This is finer than six strands of embroidery cotton, giving the flower a delicate appearance.

Sample 4 The centre has been embroidered with six strands of embroidery cotton while the outside petals are embroidered with 4 mm silk ribbon. For instructions on how to embroider a silk ribbon flower see the Superb Silks on Satin cushion project.

3

4

Effects with the basic circle

Figure 6 *Effects with the basic circle. All these samples are worked in six strands of embroidery cotton in the medium punchneedle.*

Sample a This shows the embroidery of a circle from the back of the fabric as described in Figure 5, sample 1a.

Sample b This shows the front of sample a.

Sample c This shows a domed circle. Ten stitches are punched in a circle with the punchneedle set at No 5 to form the centre. Mark the beginning for the next row (see Figure 5,

sample 1b). Change the needle length to No 3 and work all the way around the first circle as far as the beginning mark. It is not necessary to count the stitches as the work proceeds around the initial circle. Change the needle to No 1. Work all the way around the circle. Cut the thread. Domed flowers have been used in the pretty floral Mobile Phone Carriers shown on page 81.

Sample d A small flower is made with 20 stitches in a circle with the needle set at No 1. The colour has been changed and the needle lengthened to No 5, and then the centre circle has been stitched all the way around. The longer loops which are formed give the appearance of petals.

Sample e This sample has been worked the same as sample a, only the starting tag has been pulled through to the back side. It has 20 stitches in the circle. This circle can be used on the front of embroidery as an additional surface stitch.

Backstitching

Figure 7 *Backstitching can be used at the beginning and ending of a row.*

A couple of backstitches to start and finish any section of stitching can be made. Work two stitches backwards, and then stitch forward immediately on top of them. This assists in holding the first and last stitches in place. The drawback to this is that the extra stitches give added bulk to the appearance of the embroidery when only one row of stitches is worked. Where more than one row of stitches is embroidered, the extra loops get taken up within the area of the other made loops.

Special effects

There are many ways a punchneedle can be utilised to create special effects. The following samples show the diversity of the one simple stitch which make up the beauty and variety of punchneedle embroidery. Read the section on reverse punchneedle embroidery as the following stitches are all worked from the front of the fabric similarly to the versatile reverse punchneedle embroidery stitch. They are ideal for surface stitchery, where the beautiful effects of the various stitches can add an extra dimension to the creativeness of traditional punchneedle embroidery.

Sample a Reverse punchneedle embroidery

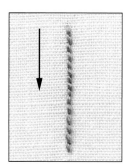

**Sample b
Closed feather stitch**

Work from the front and pull the starting thread through to the back, as for reverse punchneedle embroidery. Work forward, with one stitch. Work a stitch out and upwards to the left at approximately 45 degrees, return to the centre, and then work a stitch out and upwards to the right at approximately 45 degrees. Return to the centre and repeat the sequence. The feathery sea-green sea-fan in the project In a Coral Garden is embroidered in closed feather stitch; there, however, only one strand of thread has been used so it takes on a very different look.

Sample c Double-spaced feather stitch

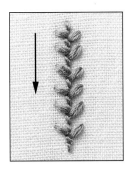

This is worked the same as sample b, but with two stitches worked forward before stitching out to the left and right.

Sample d Open feather stitch

Work with the needle set at No 2. When extending the length of the stitch on the front in the upward and outward movement, this takes away some of the loop length on the back. If the loops do not stay in place increase the length of the needle. Work from the front and pull the starting thread through to the back, as for reverse punchneedle embroidery. Work one or two straight stitches forward, then a stitch out and upwards to the left, return to the centre, work one or two straight stitches forward, depending on how far apart the stitches are required for a particular effect, and

then work a stitch out and upwards to the right, work one or two straight stitches forward, return to the centre and repeat the sequence.

Sample e Overstitching reverse punchneedle embroidery

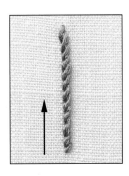

To achieve a different, more dimensional effect with reverse punchneedle embroidery, this stitch is very useful. If working in a line as shown in the sample, the stitching begins at the bottom of the line. Work one stitch backward and the next forward. This forward stitch is placed halfway along the first stitch made. The next stitch backwards is then punched into the fabric a stitch length above the top of the forward stitch. The next stitch forwards is placed almost into the same place where the forward stitch left the fabric. The backward stitch is moved gently out of the way to make way to punch in the forward stitch. If a line has been ruled, all of the stitches will enter the fabric on the same line. The stitches made appear to roll over where the needle penetrates the fabric so that you cannot see where the forward stitch was inserted. Working the stitches in this manner gives a thicker appearance to reverse punchneedle embroidery. The starting and ending threads are pulled through to the back of the fabric where they are trimmed. This stitch has been used in the Delightful Doily project.

Sample f Snail trail

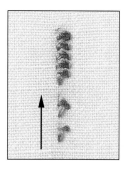

This is stitched on the front and worked backwards.

Starting at the bottom on a traced line of a design, take a small stitch backwards. Lift the needle very slightly out of the fabric, skim the needle tip over the stitch just worked and take a small horizontal stitch immediately to the right. Punch the needle into the fabric. Lift the needle tip over the stitch just made and re-insert it just above the first stitch onto the traced line. Repeat the sequence.

Sample g Open snail trail

This is stitched on the front and worked backwards.

On a traced line of a design, take a small stitch backwards. Lift the needle very slightly out of the fabric, skim the needle tip over the stitch just worked and take a small horizontal stitch immediately to the right. Punch the needle into the fabric. Lift the needle tip over the stitch just made and re-insert it just above the first stitch onto the traced line. Take a small stitch backwards before making the next horizontal stitch to give a more open look to the snail trail. This has been used in the Superb Silks on Satin cushion.

Sample h Backwards reverse punchneedle embroidery

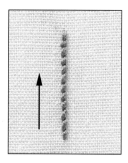

On the front of the design, work reverse punchneedle embroidery backwards, away from yourself. Doing reverse punchneedle embroidery this way gives a higher, denser appearance to the stitch. The difference in appearance is very subtle but with certain threads it becomes noticeable and interesting.

Sample i   Herringbone punch

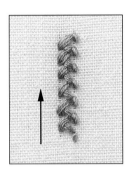

Depending on the width of the area to be embroidered, set the needle length at No 2 or 3 so that the loops hold in place. The further apart or the longer the cross-over stitches are made, the more the loop on the other side will be shortened, as some of its length is taken away by moving the needle further forward than in normal stitching. If the loop doesn't stay in place, lengthen the needle tip.

Work backwards. Begin with a small stitch backward. Then take the needle to the left at a slight upward angle. Bring a small stitch directly forward. Take the needle to the right at a slight upward angle and punch it into the fabric. Lift the needle over the stitch just made and bring a small stitch directly forward. Then take the needle to the left again at a slight upward angle.

Repeat until the required area is completed.

Sample j
Satin stitch

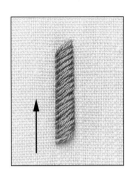

This is worked from the front with long straight stitches which are angled to the right. With this stitch it is important that the needle tip is long enough so that the punched loops stay in place on the back. When extending the length of the stitch on the front in the upward and outward movement, this takes away some of the loop length on the back. Start with the needle set at No 2; if the stitches do not hold, alter the length and keep a check on the back to see if the loops are long enough to hold in place. Hold the needle so that the bevel edge is to the left and facing at about 10 o'clock. Work the stitches close together so that the threads rest on each other to give the beautiful raised satin stitch effect known widely in traditional hand embroidery. The needle tip barely leaves the fabric as the stitches are dragged over the surface on the outward movement and then the needle tip glides over the fabric on the return inward movement.

Sample k Textured satin stitch with overlapping stitches

To work satin stitch with the slant of the stitch out to the left, it is necessary to lift the needle over the point of insertion of the previous stitch before returning to the centre to make another stitch. When lifting the needle take care as it is easy to split the fibres/strands of the thread.

Sample l Open-textured satin stitch

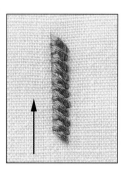

This is worked in the same way as satin stitch with overlapping stitches, except that the stitches are not punched so close together. It is possible to see where the stitches cross each other. It is used with great effect for leaves.

Sample m Open-leaf satin stitch

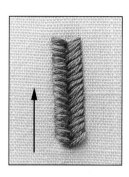

This is a great alternative for embroidering a leaf and gives quite a different look when compared to a leaf worked in satin stitch (see Figure 8).

This stitch is worked backwards. Take a stitch to the left and return to the centre. Read satin stitch with overlapping stitches above for stitching out to the left. Take a stitch to the right and return to the centre. Continue in this manner until the required area is filled in.

Sample n Open-leaf satin stitch with reverse punchneedle embroidery

Worked as above, but making the stitches to the left and the right erratic in length for a different finish. When the top or tip of the area is reached, stitch forward through the centre with small stitches in reverse punchneedle embroidery.

Satin stitch leaf

Figure 8 *Steps in embroidering a leaf in satin stitch, using three strands of embroidery cotton in the small punchneedle.*

Embroider leaves with only two or three strands of embroidery cotton with a small punchneedle, as six strands in a larger needle make leaves appear too thick and bulky.

When working a leaf in satin stitch, work from the base of the leaf to the tip. The first part of this stitching is worked backwards. When extending the length of the stitch on the front in the upward and outward movement, this takes away some of the loop length on the back, so begin with the needle set at No 2 or 3. If however, the loops do not stay in place, increase the needle length.

Turn the bevel of the needle tip slightly in your finger tips, away from the left to about 10 o'clock. Take a stitch from the centre to the right and back to the centre. Glide the back of the needle just along the former stitch. This helps to lay the stitch down smoothly. The stitching may begin to look too horizontal, in which case to get an upward angle punch a few stitches into the centre, in exactly the same hole, taking each outside stitch a little further up. Make the stitches shorter toward the tip of the leaf. At the very tip, take two or three small backward reverse punchneedle embroidery stitches to form a nice point.

The angle of the bevel when punching forward is not directly to the left, but turned in the fingers to about 8 o'clock. Moving forward, punch two or three small stitches directly over the stitches just worked. Commence stitching forward, working out to the left and then into the centre until the leaf is completed. The stitches on the left side of the leaf sit differently to those on the right.

As the tip is approached, change to a shorter needle length, which shortens the loop on the back to prevent a lot of bulk created from long loops. Lengthen the needle on its return movement on the left side. Pull the starting and finishing threads to the back of the work and trim.

Meandering stitch

Sample a Meandering stitch embroidered on the front of the fabric is simply reverse punchneedle embroidery meandering backwards,

Figure 9
Meandering stitch worked in three strands of embroidery cotton with the small punchneedle.

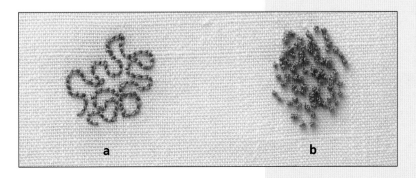

forwards, in and out and round about, leaving a delicate outline over the surface of the fabric. It is a useful fill-in surface stitch which can add great interest to a design. This has been used in a small area for the background of In a Coral Garden.

Sample b Meandering stitch worked on the back of the fabric. Where a large area is to be filled in with loops which are not close together, such as in the background of In a Coral Garden, punch from the back in the same manner as for the meandering stitch, but now the loops on the front will be random and erratic and not as uniform as when rows are worked.

Forming the perfect point

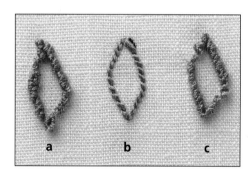

a   *b*   *c*

Figure 10 *Forming the perfect point.*

Forming the perfect point adds finesse to particular places in punchneedle embroidery. Common areas of concern for forming perfect points are the tip of a petal, pointy animal ears and the corners of a square.

Sample a Punching up to a corner or tip, stitching around it and continuing along the other side, will give an

overhanging loop which looks quite out of place.

Sample b shows the way to remedy this overhanging loop. Work along the outline tracing on the back. Stitch to the tip of a point. For the very last stitch punched at the tip, deliberately angle the needle tip inwards from the usual manner of embroidering. Punch the last stitch made at the very tip at the deliberate change to the angle. The next stitch along the second side is made longer and is punched at least one or two stitch lengths from the tip—see sample b, where a mark has been made. The sample has been exaggerated to show this. This means that on the front there is not a bunch of loops forming at the tip, all vying for a place to sit. Check on the front. It may be that a few stitches need to be undone and re-worked to achieve the perfect point, as in sample c.

Sample c shows an attractive point.

Another way to achieve a perfect point on cut-out appliqué embroidery is with the use of glue (see TIP in the section on Appliqué in Chapter 3).

Star flower

Figure 11 *Star flowers worked with six stands of embroidery cotton in the medium punchneedle.*

For surface embellishment the star flower is worked on the front of the fabric. Set the needle tip just sufficiently long enough to enable the loops to stay in place. Commence in the centre. Punch a stitch into the centre and pull the beginning thread through to the back. Make a stitch outwards to the required length and then make another stitch back into the centre. Work 5 petals for the daisy, taking each stitch in and out. Pull the end thread to the back. A small star flower is used in the project In a Coral Garden.

Stripes

In punchneedle embroidery, stripes can end up either embroidered with almost perfect delineation between the colours, or with the colours all jumbled together. There is one simple way to prevent the loops from becoming intermingled. Simply leave a space between each row.

Samples 1a and 1b show stripes where the rows have been stitched very close together. The loops on the front become so intermingled that it really seems that there are no stripes. When loops do get tangled, they can be worked over with the needle tip, separated and re-arranged.

Samples 2a and 2b show how stripes take on an almost definite line when a space has been left between the rows.

To get the very best effect for punchneedle embroidery designs such as the Jewelled Wings projects, it is important to leave a small space between each area of colour. Leaving this space gives a crisp outline between the colours. If the space is not created, the loops of the two colours become intermingled, there is no definition of line and the shape is lost.

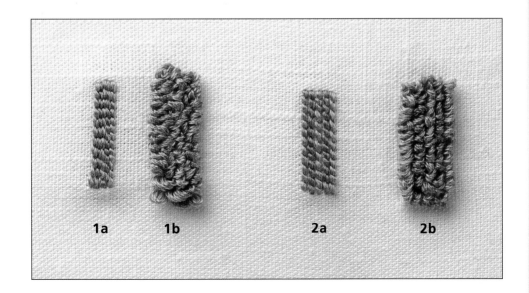

1a   **1b**   **2a**   **2b**

Figure 12 Effects
with stripes.

Blending threads

Figure 13 *This sample shows the blending of three colours using six strands of thread.*

Using different tones of the one colour through the punchneedle is just another exciting addition to punchneedle embroidery.

In Leesa's Bag, the pretty colours of the flowers and the base of the design have been blended using a mixture of three strands of thread in four tones of colour.

Blending six strands of thread

D = darkest tone, M = medium tone and L = lightest tone

The first (outer) row is worked with 6 strands of the darkest colour.

The next row, 4 strands of the dark with 2 strands of the medium.

The next row, 4 strands of medium with 2 strands of dark.

Follow this with 6 strands of medium.

Take 4 strands of medium and 2 strands of light.

The next row, 4 strands of light with 2 strands of medium.

Finally, use 6 strands of light.

To avoid distinct lines between colour changes, overlap the rows by punching a few stitches of the adjacent shade into the next shade.

Blending with three strands of thread works very well too.

Blending 6 strands of thread

6D	4D 2M	4M 2L	6M	4M 2L	4L 2M	6L

D = darkest tone
M = medium tone
L = lightest tone

Making dots

Figure 14 *How to put coloured dots over an embroidered area.*

The small square shape has been worked with six strands of embroidery cotton with the medium punchneedle set at No 1. When the needle tip is set at No 1 there is insufficient length of loop for the dots to show through the thickly textured background embroidery so to add the dots the needle length is altered to No 2. For this technique, use a gentle twisting motion of the needle through the previously formed loops. Depending on the threads used it may be necessary to hold onto the thread where it exits the fabric before punching in the next stitch. If the thread is not held in place some of the loop length is pulled out as some of its length is taken out when the needle is slid along the thread to punch in the next dot.

This technique with the dots has been used in the project Jewelled Wings 2.

Short and very short loops

Figure 15 *Short and very short loops.*

Sample a Six strands of cotton embroidered with the medium needle with the needle tip set at No 1 to make short loops.

Sample b Dots (very short loops) embroidered with a 2 mm piece of plastic on the needle tip. The short piece of plastic makes a significant difference to the length of the loop which gives a finer appearance to selected areas within a design (as seen in the project In a Coral Garden).

5. Another Dimension

There are a number of ways that dimension, texture and embellishment can be added to embroidery. Embroidering with a punchneedle in acrylic yarn gives access to a range of techniques that stand alone in their uniqueness.

Four of these techniques have been incorporated in projects for this book—sculpting, shaping, the shaggy look and fluffing.

- **Sculpting**—forming detail in the round or in relief by cutting loops.
- **Shaping**—forming shapes in the round by gradually altering the length of the loop.
- **The shaggy look**—cutting loops open to give a furry appearance.
- **Fluffing**—making a soft downy fur by brushing uncut loops with a wire brush.

Unlike the normal method of punchneedle embroidery, when working these four techniques the design is placed into the hoop upside down—that is, the embroidery is worked from within the concavity of the hoop, which is not the usual way. The trimming and brushing of the loops is thus done from the top of the hoop, where access with the scissors and the fluffing brush is easier.

In the first two of these techniques, punched loops made with 2-ply acrylic yarn are cut and contoured with sharp, pointy scissors. The result is a plush, velvet-like appearance. Although basically simple techniques, one needs time to practise to achieve the best results. These are also very forgiving techniques, because if an area is cut too much and doesn't look quite right, it is easy to remove what has been done and to re-stitch the area. Where a mistake is made and too much cutting occurs, simply embroider some more loops and trim again.

Except in the fluffing technique, after each row of loops is embroidered the

Although these two bear heads look vastly dissimilar they have been worked from exactly the same pattern. They have been embroidered in acrylic yarn and finished with the techniques of sculpting (on the left) and the shaggy look (on the right).

hoop is turned over and all of the loops are cut open by inserting the scissors into the loop, pulling the loop to its full height and then cutting through the top of each loop, not across the loops. Always cut the loops after each row otherwise the loops tangle and it becomes extremely difficult to cut them open. Working more than two rows without cutting will make it almost impossible to cut the loops as they get caught in each other. This can also be the reason why a finished sculpted area looks uneven— some cut loops may get caught up in uncut loops which themselves have been hidden underneath previously cut loops. It is easy to cut into the fabric so due care is needed when cutting the yarn.

Ensure that the fabric remains tight in the hoop while trimming, shaping, sculpting or fluffing is being done.

When acrylic yarns are cut they take on a velvety appearance and can often dramatically change colour, which can be a great advantage in some areas where only one colour is used, for example a flower petal—the change of colour adds shading, contrast and highlights. Cut loops change colour and, depending on the thread used, the colours can become richer and more vibrant. Any uncut loops remain the original colour but when cut, that yarn becomes darker and richer in colour. Where some loops escape the cutting process this can actually add character to a finished embroidery. The uncut loops remain a softer colour and add a fleck of more subtle colour into the plushness of the design.

The cutting of the fibres causes a lot of fluff and dust. Where possible, cut onto a sheet of plastic or fabric so that all the mess can be gathered up and disposed of, or sit outside to merrily sculpt, shape and fluff. Clap the hoop periodically as though playing the tambourine to remove excess filaments from the yarn.

Getting a 'good' look to sculpted areas is sometimes tricky to achieve. Take time to practise and be warned that it seems as though the trimming will go on forever—there always seems to be 'just a bit more' that needs to be tidied and trimmed. A light mist of hair spray will hold the trimmed fur in place.

The sculpting technique is wonderful for getting deep, rich and luxurious textures into punchneedle embroidery. The Bear in a Garden has been embroidered with this technique, as has the hot pink mushroom coral in In a Coral Garden.

For each of these techniques a pair of sharp, pointy-tipped scissors is necessary.

Sculpting

Sample a Shows a square marked for the embroidery.

Sample b The square has been filled in with loops with the punchneedle set at No 12.

Sample c These loops have been cut to give a shaggy look. Punch each section of the design, with stitches close together. Cut the loops as described above.

Sample d This sample shows sample c trimmed along the outside edges. Take care when trimming with the scissors as it is very easy to cut the fabric. Trimming of the edges is done

Sculpting step by step: these four samples have been embroidered with 2-ply acrylic yarn through the medium punchneedle.

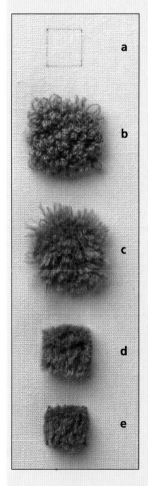

by holding the scissors absolutely vertical. Push the scissors firmly along the base of the outer row and cut off overhanging loops so that the cut edge is vertical. When the cutting of loops is complete, the area at the top will be almost the same size as the original square.

In places where too much has been cut or the finish looks patchy, punch in extra loops and then trim them.

Sample e This has been embroidered the same as sample d. It has been cut in the same manner but has had the outer, top edges rounded to give a gentle curve. To sculpt and shape like this the scissors are held at an angle to round off the top outside edges. Practise gently rolling the scissors over the surface and trimming at the same time. Trim and sculpt gently until the desired shape is achieved.

Sculpting adjoining areas

Sample a shows the embroidery from the back with a space between the two areas.

Sample b has been worked with the needle tip set at No 12. It shows the two areas from the front with the loops cut open. The space has been left the same as in sample a, however, it is not visible. Without leaving a space it is almost impossible to get the scissors between the cut yarn loops to begin the sculpting process.

Sample c shows the two areas cut, sculpted and trimmed.

Sculpting adjoining areas: where two areas side by side each require sculpting, such as body parts (see, for example, Bear in a Garden) it is necessary to leave a considerable space between them.

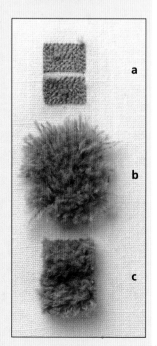

Shaping

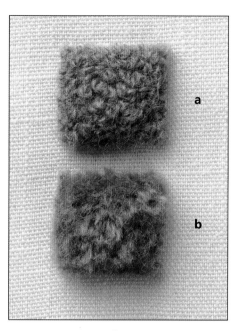

Different results are achieved with the shaping technique.

Sample a shows an area where each row has had the needle tip lengthened from No 2 through to No 9, beginning at the outside edge and working toward the centre.

Sample b this is worked in the same manner as sample a, except that the loops of each row are cut open before making the next row. This technique has been used for the Vibrant Velvet Daisies design.

Shaping, although similar to sculpting, is an easier way to get a rounded effect as it is done simply by altering the length of the needle tip for each row worked. The outside edge is worked with the needle tip set at whatever length is necessary for the required outcome. In the Vibrant Velvet Daisies embroidery, the outside edges were embroidered with the needle tip set at No 3. As each round is worked at a longer length, by the time the centre is reached, the height of the cut loops gives a thick, rounded dimension. The loops are cut after each round. As the loops are cut, the same effects on the yarn occur as mentioned previously.

Cutting in Relief

The vein on the leaf has been shaped by cutting.

Yet another dimension can be added to sculpted and shaped areas by cutting into the velvety mass, giving the distinctness of an outline. It is ideal for marking veins in leaves or defining the body parts of a bear. See the leaves in the Vibrant Velvet Daisies design.

Place the scissors in position down into the velvety mass—angle the scissors to the right and cut away some fibres. Angle the scissors to the left and cut more fibres. Check the progress and continue shaping until the required look is achieved.

Cutting in this manner makes a furrow or indent which moulds the area, allowing the design to stand out from the curved surface.

The Shaggy Look

The shaggy look is illustrated in the Bear photograph at the beginning this section and by sample c in the photograph in Sculpting above. The Shaggy Bear with a Blue Bow has also been given the shaggy look.

The shaggy look is achieved by cutting the formed loops open. After each row of loops is embroidered, the hoop is turned over and all the loops are cut open by inserting the scissors into the loop, pulling the loop to its full height and then cutting through the top of each loop, not across the loops. As well, it is important that the scissors are not held at an angle whereby the cut loops become uneven with one side longer than the other, giving rise to uneven loops and an uneven, unattractive surface. Always cut the loops after each row otherwise the loops tangle and it becomes extremely difficult to cut them open. Working more than two rows without cutting will make it almost impossible to cut the loops, as they get caught in each other and it is difficult to pull them to their full height to get the point of the scissors through the loop at the very top. This can also be the reason for the shaggy look becoming unattractively untidy.

Fluffing

Acrylic yarn after brushing with the fluffing brush.

Fluffing is the technique used for the project Patch the Fluffy Dog.

The brushing of acrylic yarn with a wire-bristled fluffing brush (see photograph) results in a soft, downy, furry effect which is ideal for a Santa's beard, and the coats of cats and dogs.

The formed loops are *not cut* before brushing. The stitching on the back can be glued and left to dry before starting to brush, but this is not necessary.

The fluffing brush.

When beginning and ending any area that is to be fluffed, backstitch (see Stitch Glossary, Figure 7) directly over the three previous stitches *or* leave a long length of thread at the beginning and end. The reason for this is that when the brushing is being done, the beginning and end yarn can very easily get caught in the bristles of the fluffing brush and some stitches can be pulled out. The long pieces of yarn are held in place with a finger on the back of the embroidery during the brushing process to prevent their being snagged and pulled. They are trimmed later. If however, a long end of thread does become unstitched during the brushing process, trim it before going on with any further brushing and then hold it in place on the back when brushing is resumed.

It is best that the brushing is done while the fabric is held tightly in the hoop. Turn the hoop over so that the flat surface of the fabric is uppermost for ease of brushing.

The risk of damaging the fabric with the wire bristles of the fluffing brush can be overcome by the use of small pieces of masking tape shaped and pressed along the marked outline which will protect the fabric from the metal teeth of the wire brush. A second row of tape may be required to increase the width.

Only a small section is punched at the one time. This is brushed before going on to the next section. Punch and brush in a progressive manner. That is, work from one side to the other; instead of for instance, punching in all of one colour first. All fluffy areas are worked and brushed before any non-brushed areas such as a nose or eyes are worked.

A stab from the wire bristles into fingers is painful. Work safely.

When brushing, hold the brush firmly by the wooden handle with the wire bristles bent toward you. Press the brush firmly into the loops and drag the bristles through the loops.

Feel deep into the stitching with your fingers to check that all loops have been brushed out. Any lumps that can be felt indicate areas that have not been brushed sufficiently deeply. Turn the work and brush in all directions.

To complete the process, angle the bent bristles into the downy fur, especially at the edges, and brush further.

If the brushing process is over-zealous the thickness of the yarn in the stitches on the back gets much thinner. It can happen that fibres of the yarn will be dragged out of the fabric, resulting in a sparse coverage of fluff.

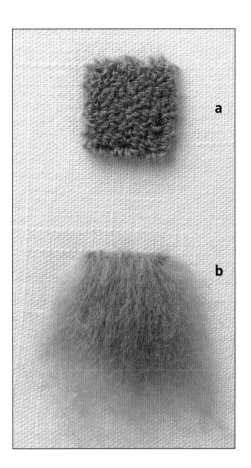

Fluffing: before and after brushing.

Sample a The loops have been punched with the needle tip set at No 3.

Sample b Shows sample a after it has been brushed.

Loops made with the needle tip set at No 3 will brush out to make a downy fur about 4–5 cm (2 in) in length.

Loops made with the needle tip set at No 12 will brush out to give a staple about 8 cm (3 in) in length.

PROBLEM SOLVING

Frequently, 'things' happen that prevent the loops of punchneedle embroidery from holding in place or the piece of embroidery does not look 'good' when completed. There are many reasons why this occurs. Read through the following guide to learn how to improve your technique and work out why punched loops are not staying in the fabric.

◆ It is a two-part process to thread the needle. Firstly, check that the thread is passed through the punchneedle handle and the bore of the needle, secondly, that it is threaded through the eye of the needle.

◆ Check that the thread is flowing freely. The thread flows from the end of the punchneedle over the wrist so that the arm is not resting on the thread. Take care that the thread is not wrapped around your fingers or being held alongside the needle. It is easy for the thread to get caught on something preventing it from flowing freely. If the thread is not flowing, a loop is unable to form.

◆ During the punching process, if the needle is lifted clear of the fabric and not closely

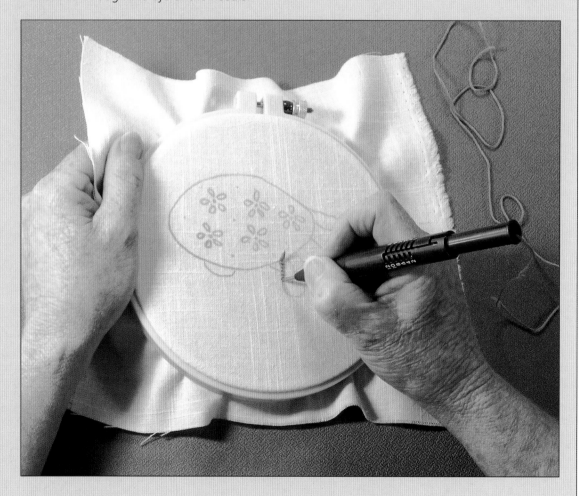

skimmed across the surface, the loops previously made will be pulled out from the front of the fabric of the fabric.

◆ When all of the above have been checked, it may be necessary to cut the thread, and take the punchneedle apart to see if something is amiss inside the punchneedle itself. There are times when a knot or clump of thread is pulled into the handle and then that is unable to pass through the bore of the needle. It may be that a thread from a frayed edge of the fabric (it is a good idea to overlock or tape any frayed edges), or another piece of thread can attach to the thread being used. When these all pass together through the needle they can clog up the bore.

◆ If the needle tip is not long enough then a sufficiently long loop is not formed on the front to stay in the fabric. When loops are too short they cannot stay in place.

◆ When things aren't progressing, the most important issue is whether the fabric is tight enough in the hoop (see Hoop Techniques in Chapter 3). When the entire list above has been worked through, check the fabric in the hoop. With loose, baggy fabric in the hoop, loops of punchneedle embroidery are unable to form properly.

◆ When the incorrect thread thickness has been chosen for a particular size needle, either the thread is too thick to flow through the needle, or it is too fine, when it simply runs through the needle too quickly.

◆ The needle tip needs to be travelling forward. If inadvertently you are stitching backwards it is easy to punch the needle through the thread, cutting and shredding it.

◆ The stitches on the back are usually spaced about a needle-width apart. Where a short needle length is set and the running stitches on the back are spaced too far apart, some of the loop length will be taken up on the back of the work as a straight stitch and the loops will not be long enough to stay in place.

◆ Where a lot of unpicking has been done, the fibres of the fabric can become fragile, and even severely damaged. It is the weave of the fabric which holds the loops in place. When the weave is damaged, the loops cannot possibly be held in place. Try some iron-on woven interfacing behind the damaged fabric to overcome this (see Iron-on Interfacing in Chapter 2).

◆ Uneven lengths of loop on the front side of the embroidery can simply be that the fabric is not tight enough in the hoop.

◆ Check the weave of the fabric. Loops cannot stay in place if the weave of the fabric is too open as it is the weave of the fabric which holds the loop in place.

◆ As well if the needle tip is not punched to its full depth on each punch then the loops on the front will be uneven in length.

◆ A patchy look on the front can be that the loops have not been embroidered closely enough together or the rows are too far apart.

◆ When the embroidery is removed from the hoop and it curls this can be an indication that the stitching of the punched loops has been too close.

◆ Adjoining colours becoming intermingled can be remedied by leaving a space between the two rows of colour.

LOVELY LAVENDER

This small embroidery has been designed to fit into an oval-cut, tri-fold card, making it a great gift to give to a friend. The simple technique of punchneedle embroidery which is easy to learn lends itself well to this charming lavender design.

Materials

medium punchneedle

15 cm lip-lock embroidery hoop

25 cm (9 in) square of woven fabric,
*   polyester/viscose/flax blend is ideal*

rainbow-coloured iron-on transfer paper (see
*   Chapter 3 Techniques); alternatively, the fabric*
*   can be lightly coloured with pencils or paint*

plus the materials listed in the box: Mounting an
*   Embroidery in an Oval-cut Card*

Threads

Rajmahal Art Silk
   dainty lilac 111
   purple dusk 113
   Madeira six-stranded embroidery cotton green
   1513

TIP

In this design there are a number of places where the embroidery is worked from the front of the piece. These areas are marked on the pattern as lines of dashes. It is called reverse punchneedle embroidery (see Stitch Glossary, Figure 3) whereby the beautiful little running stitch that is normally worked on the back of the fabric is embroidered on the front. The loops are then formed on the back of the fabric. Reverse punchneedle embroidery emulates the traditional embroidery stitch known as 'stem-stitch'.

Tracing guide

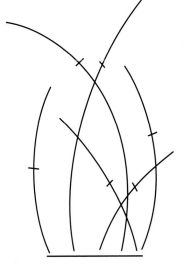

Stitching guide

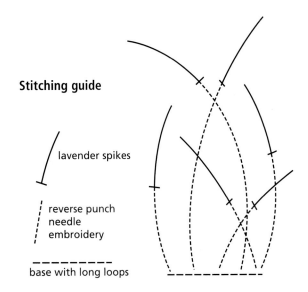

lavender spikes

reverse punch needle embroidery

base with long loops

Background colour guide

This diagram indicates the background lavenders drawn with colour pencils

Preparation

Iron a square of the coloured transfer paper onto the front and in the centre of the fabric.

Check the stretch of the fabric and place the design upright with the most stretch of the fabric going up and down.

Transfer the design on to the back of the fabric (see Chapter 3 Techniques).

The stems are embroidered from the front of the fabric in reverse punchneedle embroidery (see Stitch Glossary, Figure 3b). To mark the placement for the stems onto the front of the fabric, in preparation for reverse punchneedle embroidery, turn the fabric over, hold it up to a window or over a light box and trace the required outlines onto the front of the fabric.

Assemble the fabric very tightly in the hoop.

Embroidery

Use six strands of thread throughout.

Lavender spikes

Follow the step-by-step diagrams and instructions shown on the pattern to embroider the lavender spikes.

Set the punchneedle at No 2 and with six strands of pale mauve, work 13 stitches in a row starting from the mark indicated on each lavender spike. Turn the design in the hoop so that you are stitching forward. Work in the direction of the arrow (diagram 1). Read Direction of Work, page 31.

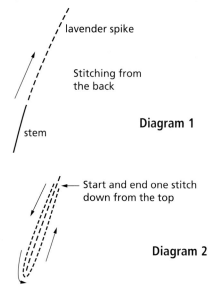

lavender spike

Stitching from the back

stem

Diagram 1

Start and end one stitch down from the top

Diagram 2

Change the needle tip to No 1 and, still with six strands of the pale mauve, start near the top of the first row but one stitch down from the top, close to the first row, and work all the way around the first row, stopping one stitch down from the top (diagram 2). Work in the direction of the arrow. Work as many stitches around the

first row as needed, it is not necessary to count them.

With the needle still set at No 1, change to dark mauve and six strands. Punch the lavender tip (diagram 3) with the stitches close together and work the tip in a V-shape using the diagram as a guide. Check the front of the work and if there are spaces in the tip, work in some more loops. Check the front to see that the tips look tidy.

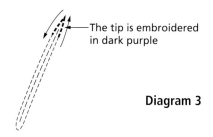

The tip is embroidered in dark purple

Diagram 3

Stems

The stems are embroidered in reverse punchneedle embroidery on the front of the fabric (see Stitch Glossary, Figure 3).

Set the needle tip at No 1 and use six strands of the green thread. Remember to take beginning and the end threads through to the back of the fabric.

Long grass at base of the lavender

Work with six strands of green thread.

Work along the traced line at the base of the lavender stems on the back of the fabric. The tufts are made with very long loops. The very long loops are made with the needle tip measured at 4.7 cm (1 ⅞ in). When using the Ultra-Punchneedle remove the casing and spring from the medium needle tip and handle (see Long Loops, page 16). Store these away safely. The very long loops are made with the full length of the exposed needle tip. Punch the very long needle tip all the way to the blue of the handle. Work along the marked line from the back of the fabric.

To get the long grass to stand upright, a row of reverse punch stitching is made across the loops, 2 mm up from the base of the loops. To do this replace the casing, set the punchneedle at No 2 and from the front, work over the long loops with reverse punchneedle embroidery, 2 mm up from the base of the loops. See diagram 4.

Stitching on the front is worked over the loops

Diagram 4

Cut the long loops unevenly to give a tufted grass effect.

Turn the piece over and, working from the back with the punchneedle set at No 2, stitch two rows underneath the row of reverse punchneedle embroidery. Cut these loops at the front (see photograph).

Finishing

Before removing the fabric from the hoop, take a green, mauve and pink coloured pencil and lightly colour in some background lavender (see photograph). This step is optional.

Remove the fabric from the hoop and stretch in all directions to straighten out the grain of the fabric.

Assemble this delightful embroidery into a tri-fold card as described in the box: Mounting an Embroidery into an Oval-cut Card.

MOUNTING AN EMBROIDERY INTO AN OVAL-CUT CARD

Requirements

tri-fold oval cut-out card

plastic oval dome to fit into the card

water-erasable pen

sharp scissors

glue stick or 2-sided tape

small piece of cardboard, 9 x 12 cm (3 ½ x 4 in) that is cut the same size as the plastic dome

small piece of pellon, 9 x 12 cm (3 ½ x 4 in)

3D foam tape: 6 mm (¼ in) squares

Assembly

Position the pellon into place over the cardboard with a small piece of two sided tape and set aside.

Temporarily position the plastic dome in place over the finished embroidery and with the water-erasable pen draw the outline of the plastic dome, making sure to mark the four corners well. Remove the dome.

Cut the fabric away from the long sides of the drawn outline of the dome so that there is only about a 4 cm (1 ½ in) fabric allowance remaining.

Put two-sided tape along both of the long sides on the back of the cardboard.

At this stage place a clean, soft cloth over the work area, which will both protect the embroidery and prevent the plastic dome from being scratched.

Place the fabric with the right side of the embroidery facing down onto the table top. With the pellon facing down, place the pellon-covered cardboard over the back of the embroidery, matching the corners of the

cardboard to the corners drawn on the fabric. Bring the fabric allowance from the long sides over the cardboard, align the water-erasable pen marks with the side of the cardboard and pull the fabric allowance over the two-sided tape (protective coating removed) which will then hold fabric in position.

Make sure that the embroidery looks straight in its position on the card.

Cut off the excess fabric at the top and bottom in line with the card.

Adhere a small piece of two-sided tape on two diagonal corners on the back of the plastic dome and then place the plastic dome into position over the front of the embroidery. Press down to secure in place.

Put two-sided tape on the top and bottom edges on the front of the dome and position the oval-cut card over the dome, pressing securely into place.

On the centre section of the card where the embroidery has been mounted, stick three small pieces of foam tape along the top and bottom edge of the card and one piece in the centre of the right edge—opposite the fold of the card.

Fold the card and firmly press the edges together. Depending on the thickness of the cardboard and the embroidery, two pieces of foam stuck together at the middle foam square position may be necessary to accommodate the bulk.

Placing the dome into the card is the perfect way to protect a small piece of punchneedle embroidery. The card becomes a great gift to give to a dear friend.

Make sure to sign the card.

PURPLE POTTED BLOOMS

This simple but lovely design is made up of small circles of punched loops which when massed together resemble beautiful mauve-purple flowers. Mounted into a card, this becomes the perfect long lasting gift for any occasion.

Materials

medium punchneedle

15 cm lip-lock embroidery hoop

threads—Rajmahal art silks

25 cm (9 in) square of fabric

small terracotta pot, half-round, 2.5 cm high and
2.5 cm across the top (1 in x 1 in)

fine, sharp, pointy scissors

You Can Wash It craft glue

small piece of two-sided tape

plus the requirements listed in the previous
project in the box: Mounting an Embroidery
into an Oval-cut Card.

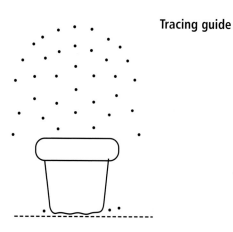

Tracing guide

Threads

Rajmahal Art Silk
  dainty lilac 111
  purple dusk 113
  green earth 421

Preparation

Trace the design on to the back of the fabric.

Place the fabric in the hoop with the traced design uppermost. Ensure that the fabric is extremely taut in the hoop.

A medium punchneedle with six strands of Rajmahal thread is used.

TIP

The terracotta pot is not glued into position until the completion of the embroidery as the needle tip may be damaged if scraped along the top of the pot when punching.

Embroidery

Flowers

This design is made up of small circles which when massed together resemble beautiful flowers. To form each flower, work in a circle

	No	Stitches
⊗	6	8—421
⊠	8	4—421
⊙	8	10—113
✕	8	6—421
∅	6	8—3 strands of 113 and 3 strands of 111 together
●	6	8—113
◉	5	8—111
✳	4	5—421
●	4	4—111
▪	3	4—113
⌀	3	4—111

Colour guide

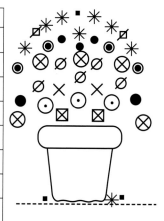

Rajmahal art silk
421—green earth
111—dainty lilac
113—purple dusk

(see Stitch Glossary, Figure 5). Follow the legend shown on the pattern for the placement of colours.

To form a flower use whatever colour and length of loop is indicated on the pattern for each individual flower. Where the pattern indicates for example, No 8 and 8 stitches, this means to set the needle at No 8 and work 8 stitches around in a circle. Commence each circle by punching directly into the centre of each symbol and then work the circle with the required number of stitches.

TIP

Adhere the two-sided tape to the back of the terracotta pot and place the pot temporarily into position to check for balance of the design as the work progresses.

Note that there are some flowers which are embroidered with three strands of the dark and the pale mauve colours threaded together through the medium punchneedle.

When the flowers and greenery in the pot have been completed, embroider the small petals at the base of the pot where indicated on the pattern. Look at the photograph to see where to put in the base line.

The base line is worked with the green thread with the needle tip set at No 1 in reverse punchneedle embroidery (see Stitch Glossary, Figure 3b) from the front of the fabric. Reverse punchneedle embroidery, worked on the front of the fabric, is a wonderful, decorative surface stitch which adds another dimension to punchneedle embroidery. Remember to take the beginning and ending threads of this row through to the back of the embroidery.

Tidy up the back of the work by trimming the threads.

TIP

It helps when working a small floral design to view the embroidery in a mirror to see it in reverse, and also held upside down. This helps to clarify points of imbalance or any other faults which were not previously obvious. Again this gives a realistic idea of the overall balance. Add more loops where needed.

Note that darker colours are used at the base of the design near to the top of the pot. Using darker colours at the base of the design help to ground it. Gradually changing to paler colours toward the top prevents a top-heavy appearance.

The final stage of the embroidery is to put in the tiny area of green and the fallen mauve blossoms at the base of the pot (see pattern).

Finishing

Remove the temporarily placed terracotta pot and remove the tape. Take a length of dark mauve thread and wrap it around the pot as seen in the photograph. Secure it by applying a small amount of glue to the thread on back of the pot. Set aside to dry.

Remove the fabric from the hoop and stretch in all directions to straighten out the grain.

Glue the pot carefully into position, taking care that no glue gets on the embroidery.

Assemble this delightful embroidery into a card following the instructions in Mounting an Embroidery into an Oval-cut Card.

What a lovely gift for a special friend.

MOBILE PHONE CARRIERS

These delightful covers are an attractive way to protect mobile phones. There are two different styles which make great fashion accessories—an appealing floral and a stylish black. The flower garden is embroidered with pretty cottons while the black abstract piece has been worked with dramatic cotton colours.

Materials

small and medium punchneedles

15 cm (6 in) lip-lock hoop

22 cm (9 in) square of good quality fabric (if you are working on a designer fabric it may be necessary to adhere an iron-on interfacing to the back of it; see Chapter 3 Techniques)

sharp embroidery scissors

fine steel crochet hook

iron-on transfer pen

Black background design

Threads

	DMC	Madeira
green	910	1303
blue	796	913
red	498	704
orange	970	203
gold	781	2212
purple	550	2709
peacock	3812	2705
teal	943	2706
black		
magenta	915	705
metallic gold	5282	5014

Preparation

Trace the design onto the back of the fabric.

Place the fabric in the hoop with the traced design uppermost. Ensure that the fabric is extremely tight in the hoop.

Embroidery

Take a good look at the colour photograph to see the placement for the colours.

Use the small punchneedle with three strands of thread.

Set the punchneedle at No 1. Follow the colours indicated on the pattern.

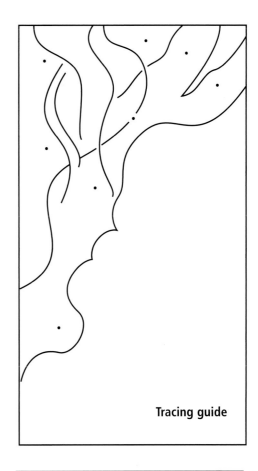

Tracing guide

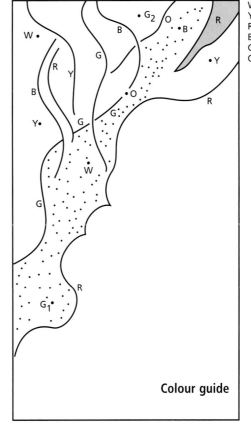

W	white
Y	yellow
R	red
B	blue
G	green
O	orange

Colour guide

The circles The four small circles towards the top in white, green, blue and yellow are worked with 10 stitches in a circle (see Stitch Glossary, Figure 5).

The other yellow and white circles are worked with 15 stitches in a circle.

The orange circle is worked with 20 stitches in a circle.

The green circle at the bottom is worked with 30 stitches in a circle.

The random dots are worked with orange, red, green, yellow and blue with the punchneedle set at No 2 (see Stitch Glossary, Figure 14).

Embroider the red outline with the stitches quite close together.

Embroider the colours as shown on the pattern.

TIP

To get the very best effect with this design, it is important to leave a small space between each area of colour. Leaving this space gives a crisp outline between the colours. If the space is not created the loops of the two colours become intermingled, and then there is no definition of line and the shape is lost.

Finishing

Check the completed piece to see that all of the loops on the front are even. Carefully use the crochet hook to pull longer loops through to the back if necessary.

Remove the fabric from the hoop. Pull the fabric into shape. Trim the ends of the threads on the back.

Floral design

Threads

	Madeira	DMC
hot pink	703	60
dark pinky-mauve	708	3607
dark pink	701	602
light mauvy-pink	710	3609
mauve	803	209
yellow	109	726
white	2403	3865
light blue	907	794
dark green	1601	3362
bright green	1502	470
black	2400	310

The direct DMC to Madeira colour conversions often are not totally correct for a specific design. In this instance coordinated colours have been chosen to give the best effect for the design.

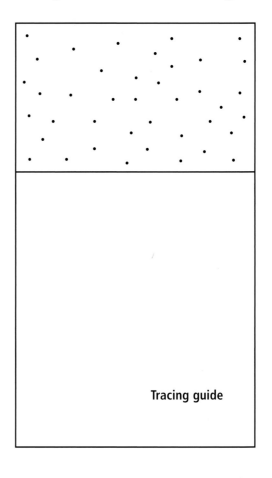

Tracing guide

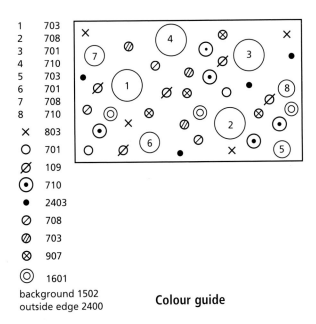

1	703
2	708
3	701
4	710
5	703
6	701
7	708
8	710
✕	803
○	701
∅	109
⊙	710
●	2403
⊘	708
⊘	703
⊗	907
◎	1601

background 1502
outside edge 2400

Colour guide

Preparation

Refer to page 79.

Embroidery

Use the medium punchneedle with six strands of cotton.

Take a good look at the colour photograph to see the placement for the colours.

Embroider the colours as indicated on the pattern. Each small flower is worked with 10 stitches in a circle.

Flower numbers 1, 2, 3 and 4 are worked as a dome, seen in Stitch Glossary, Figure 6, sample c. To work these flowers set the punchneedle at No 3 and work 20 stitches in a circle. Change the needle tip to No 2 and work all around the circle. Set the punchneedle at No 1 and work all the way around the circle.

Flower numbers 5, 6, 7 and 8 Set the punchneedle at No 3 and work 20 stitches in a circle. Change the needle tip to No 2 and work all around the circle.

Fill in the background with the bright green.

Embroider one row of black around the outside edges, working with the stitches very close together.

Finishing

Refer to page 80.

TIP

As the mobile phone cover will possibly take lots of wear and tear it is advisable to smear You Can Wash It craft glue over the back of the embroidery to prevent the loops from pulling out accidentally if they get caught on things such as car keys, etc. Leave the piece to dry.

Make these carrying cases using a preferred method for assembling a soft fabric case. Refer to box, Instructions for Making a Mobile Phone Carrier, and adorn them with beads and hand-made cords (see Chapter 3 Techniques for making cords).

MAKING A MOBILE PHONE CARRIER

The top of the hand towel (see A Hen with her Friend) and the hot water bottle cover (see A Floral Bouquet in Wool) are made in similar fashion.

Fabric required

mobile phone carrier 15 x 23 cm (6 x 9 in)

top for a hand towel 53 x 25 cm (21 x 10 in)

hot water bottle cover 61 x 46 cm (24 x 18 in);
it may be necessary to piece the fabric to
make this size; similar amount of wadding

Making up

When the embroidery is completed, remove it from the hoop and iron the fabric. Cut the fabric to the required size. Put sides A and B right side together, and stitch, leaving a 6 mm (¼ in) seam allowance (diagram 1).

Take the seam and position in the middle at the back (diagram 2), taking care that the embroidery is centred on the front.

Turn the right way out. Turn in the bottom seam allowance and hand stitch.

On the fold line, fold the fabric inside the bag to form a lining.

Cords, beads and bows can be stitched into place but are optional.

Notes for the hand towel

The bottom seam allowance for the towel top is not stitched together but stitched onto a handtowel, which is folded to fit inside the sleeve of fabric. The top edge is folded in and hand-stitched to neaten the edge. A button and buttonhole, press stud or Velcro can be used for the fastener.

Notes for the hot water bottle cover

With the hot water bottle cover, before folding over the lining cut wadding to size and place between the two layers. A cuff with a cord trim can be added to the top of the cover.

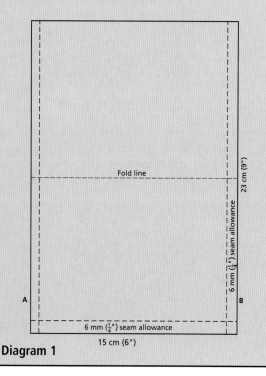

Diagram 1

Fold line

23 cm (9")

6 mm (¼") seam allowance

A

B

6 mm (¼") seam allowance

15 cm (6")

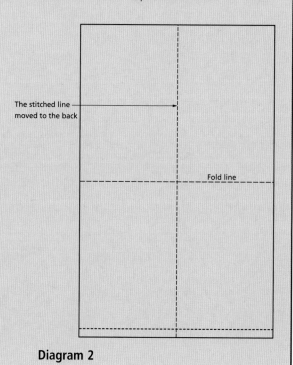

Diagram 2

The stitched line moved to the back

Fold line

A HEN WITH HER FRIEND

Add charm to hand towels with an adorable hen with her friend, the majestic
rooster, both embroidered in a variety of enchanting tones with three strands of
cotton. The perfect addition to any country-look kitchen.

Requirements

small punchneedle

15 cm (6 in) lip-lock embroidery hoop

25 cm (10 in) square of fabric to coordinate with chosen hand towel

iron-on transfer pen

You Can Wash it craft glue

sewing needle

Threads

	Madeira	DMC
pale beige	*2209*	*729*
ochre	*2010*	*680*
rust	*2302*	*976*
mid brown	*2008*	*433*
chestnut	*2304*	*400*
dark brown	*2005*	*938*
dull red	*2502*	*3777*
beige	*2011*	*436*
very light beige	*2103*	*3828*
green	*1313*	*319*
emerald	*2704*	*3818*
mid grey	*1813*	*647*
pale grey	*1804*	*762*

Preparation

Trace the design onto the back of the fabric.

Assemble the fabric very tightly in the hoop with the traced design uppermost.

Embroidery

Use three strands of thread. Set the punchneedle at No 1.

Work the outside edges with the stitches very close together.

Follow the colour placement and fill in each area as shown on the pattern.

Legs and feet

The legs are worked with two rows of stitches close together.

When embroidering the feet, punch in only one row of loops for the toes. When these have been worked, they will look like a mass of indistinguishable loops (see photograph).

The way to separate each toe is to use a tiny dab of glue on the tip of a pin. Put the glue on either side of the loops of a toe and gently push the loops together with your fingers or the pin.

This takes time but it is one way to add finesse

Tracing guides

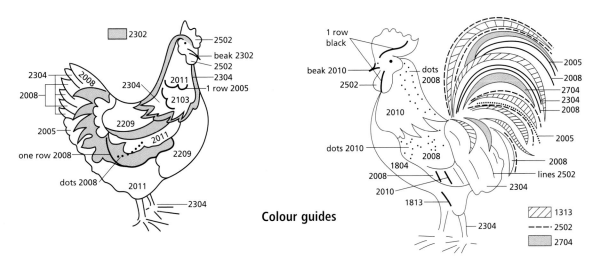

Colour guides

The hen's toes before the loops are separated.

to a piece of punchneedle embroidery in cases where the loops bunch together and give no shape.

Alternatively, use reverse punchneedle embroidery (see Stitch Glossary, Figure 3) for the feet. Embroidering the feet in the reverse gives a finer, more delicate look, as seen in the second photograph.

The hen's toes embroidered in reverse punchneedle embroidery.

Beak

Work only two rows for the beak and when finished put a little glue on each edge. Press the loops together to form a sharp point.

Alternatively, the beak can be embroidered in reverse punchneedle embroidery.

Dots

See the pattern for areas of dots to be embroidered. These are made by setting the needle tip at No 2. They are worked randomly but not too close together. They are worked by twisting the needle tip through the embroidered areas (see Stitch Glossary, Figure 14).

Eyes

These are put in with a needle and thread. Thread a short length of three strands of black and tie a very firm knot at the end. Trim any extending end thread very close to the knot. Pull on the knot to ensure that it will not come undone. Pass the needle from the front to the back at the point indicated for the eye on the pattern and allow the knot to settle into place just above the loops. Secure the thread at the back.

Finishing

Remove the piece from the hoop. Stretch the fabric in all directions and press around the embroidery.

Make this delightful design into the top of a kitchen hand towel (see box in previous project: Making a Mobile Phone Carrier).

A FLORAL BOUQUET IN WOOL

Wool embroidery is an old-time favourite and it looks superb when worked with a punchneedle, where various textures and depths are easily created. This lovely floral design lends itself well to a much-loved hot-water bottle cover (or heat-bead wrap) for cosy winter nights. Equally, the floral bouquet looks splendid on a knee rug or stylishly framed.

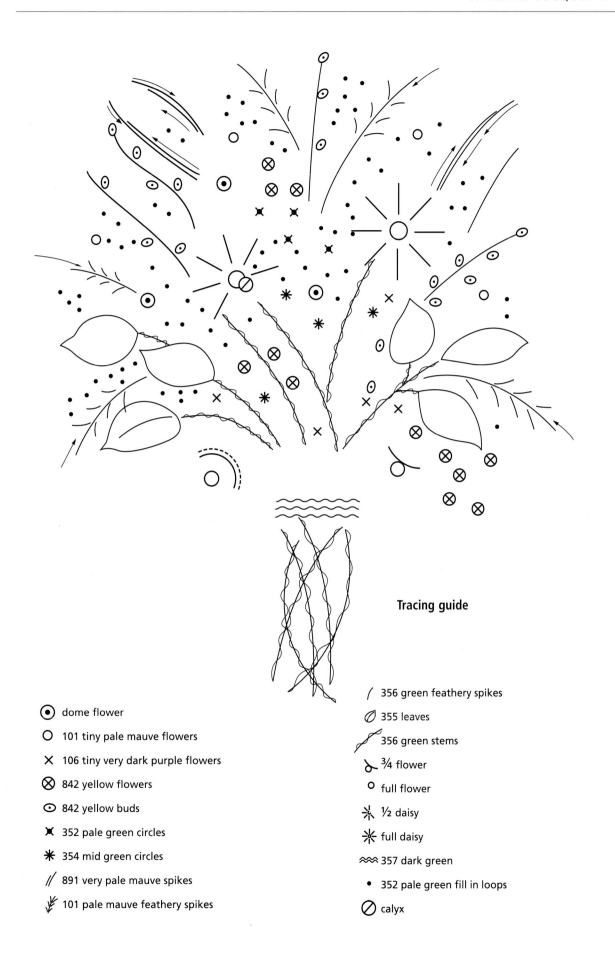

Tracing guide

- ⊙ dome flower
- ○ 101 tiny pale mauve flowers
- ✕ 106 tiny very dark purple flowers
- ⊗ 842 yellow flowers
- ⊙ 842 yellow buds
- ✕ 352 pale green circles
- ✳ 354 mid green circles
- ∥ 891 very pale mauve spikes
- ⚕ 101 pale mauve feathery spikes

- ∕ 356 green feathery spikes
- ⌀ 355 leaves
- ⌀ 356 green stems
- ⅄ ¾ flower
- ○ full flower
- ⚘ ½ daisy
- ✳ full daisy
- ∾∾ 357 dark green
- • 352 pale green fill in loops
- ⊘ calyx

Requirements

large and medium punchneedles

25 cm (10 in) lip-lock embroidery hoop

woven wool fabric (doctor's flannel is ideal as it is
not as thick as woollen blanketing); the
finished size for making up needs to be
61 x 46 cm (24 x 18 in) if using the given
instructions for assembly; alternatively, extra
fabric can be stitched around the embroidery
on completion

iron-on transfer pen

needle and thread for stitching the bow in place

green and pale mauve 9 mm organza ribbon for
bow (optional)

Threads

Appleton's tapestry and crewel embroidery wool
have been chosen for this design.

TIP

Interestingly, some brands of tapestry wool do not work
at all well through the large punchneedle. Be aware of
this if you choose an alternative to Appleton's tapestry
wool.

Appleton's tapestry wool	Crewel wool
pale mauve 101	very pale mauve 891
mid mauve 102	pale mauve 101
dark mauve 104	mid mauve 102
purple 105	very dark purple 106
paler green 355	green 356
mid green 356	mid green 354
dark green 357	pale green 352
yellow 842	

Preparation

Trace the design onto the back of the fabric.

Before commencing this project read the
section on woollen fabrics in Requirements.

TIP

The easiest method for getting a design onto fabric is
with an iron-on transfer pen (see Transferring a Design
in Chapter 3 Techniques).

As the floral bouquet is to be embroidered onto a
woollen fabric the heat of the iron needs to be
considered as it can damage and scorch the fibres
of the wool. Due care is required to prevent any
damage to the woollen fabric. Use the
appropriate setting on the iron for wool. Warm
the ironing board very well, which will assist in
hurrying along the transfer process. Warm the
fabric by gliding the iron gently over it a few
times. As the iron will not be as hot as is
generally required to transfer the design it might
take a little longer for the image to transfer onto
the fabric.

With the design transferred, assemble the
fabric very tightly in the hoop with the traced
design uppermost.

Embroidery

Use the large punchneedle for the tapestry wool
and the medium punchneedle for the crewel
wool.

Full flower

This technique is illustrated step-by-step in the
Stitch Glossary (Figure 5).

This flower is worked in tapestry wool.

Centre—pale mauve 101, in the large
punchneedle. Set the punchneedle at No 3 and
work 20 stitches in a circle.

Change to mid mauve 102, set the
punchneedle at No 5 and work all the way
around the centre.

Change to dark mauve 104, set the
punchneedle at No 8 and work all the way
around the previous row.

Change to purple 105, and with the needle set at No 11 work all the way around the previous row.

The next stage is to work only halfway around the flower on the area indicated as a line on the pattern above the flower. Use the purple and the needle at No 11.

Finally, set the needle at No 2 and with the purple punch in the short loops indicated on the pattern with a dotted line. This row is worked close to the previous row of long loops.

TIP

Why work halfway around the flower and then punch in short loops? When a big flower is embroidered it can look as though it is facing directly forward which artistically does not look so good. Working a row halfway around begins to give the flower the appearance of a slight tilt. When the final short loops are put in place the loops hold the petals up, thus giving an even more tilted look. This makes the completed flower look even more realistic.

Yellow dots into the centre of flower

See Stitch Glossary, Figure 14, for making dots. Set the punchneedle at No 5 and with yellow 842, gently punch through the pale mauve loops of the centre and make 4–5 dots (loops) of yellow (see Figure 14).

Three-quarter flower

This flower is worked in tapestry wool.

Work the centre the same as the full flower.

This flower is only worked three-quarters of the way around the centre, as indicated by the mark on the pattern.

Continue to work the same colour changes and needle lengths as the full flower, only until and including the first row of purple. Punch yellow dots in the centre.

Full daisy

This flower is worked in tapestry wool.

Centre—yellow 842. Set the punchneedle at No 6 and work five stitches in a circle (see Stitch Glossary, Figure 5).

There are nine spokes to the daisy and each spoke is worked similarly. Set the punchneedle at No 6 and with mid mauve 102, make four stitches.

Change to dark purple 104, and set the punchneedle at No 4. Stitch around the four stitches already made, working up one side and down the other (see diagram 1 for direction of stitching, and read Making Perfect Points in Chapter 3 Techniques).

Diagram 1
Full daisy petals

TIP

When working with wool or thicker thread, the stitches made at the point of each petal are further apart so that the loops on the front are not so close together, which helps in giving a sharper point to the petal tips. Turn the work over to check the front, as it might be that either further loops will need to be embroidered or some loops will need to be removed to give a better look to the points of the petals.

Half daisy

This flower is worked in tapestry wool.

The **calyx** (the green area where the petals are attached) is worked in green crewel wool 365. Set the punchneedle at No 5 and work eight stitches in a circle.

Petals Work in mid mauve tapestry wool 102.

Each spoke is made by starting at the calyx and working six stitches outward, and five stitches back toward the calyx (see diagram 2).

Diagram 2
Half daisy petals

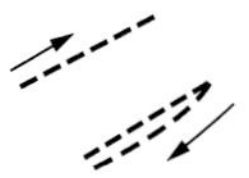

Leaves These are worked in tapestry wool. Set the punchneedle at No 2 and with paler green 355, fill in the leaf areas.

Dome flowers

These are worked with tapestry wool. There are three dome flowers and they are all embroidered the same.

Set the punchneedle at No 7 and with pale mauve 101, work 5 stitches in a circle (see Stitch Glossary, Figure 6).

Set the punchneedle at No 6 and with mid mauve 102, work all the way around the centre.

Set the punchneedle at No 5 and with dark mauve 104, work all the way around the previous row.

Mauve feathery spikes

These spikes are worked similarly to feather stitch (see Special Effects, sample b, p52).

These are worked in crewel wool.

Use the pale mauve 101. Set the punchneedle at No 2. Work in the direction of the arrow shown on the pattern. Turn the hoop and position the design so that you are embroidering forward. (See Direction of Work.) The method for embroidery of these feathery spikes is to embroider four stitches forward, and then work three or four stitches out to the left and up at an angle.

Return to the centre line by working directly over the stitches that have previously been embroidered. Embroider three or four stitches out and up at an angle to the right, then return to the centre line.

Embroider four stitches forward and repeat the stitching out to the left and right and forward for the length of the spike.

Green feathery spikes

These are worked in crewel wool in the same manner as the mauve feathery spikes, with mid green 356.

Yellow flower buds along the green spike are worked in tapestry wool yellow 842. The placement for the buds is shown on the pattern. The buds are made with the needle tip set at No 3. Depending on the position of the buds, they can be embroidered with two, three or four loops close together. At the tip only use one or two loops. Further along the spike add more loops.

Yellow flowers

These are worked in tapestry wool, yellow 842.

Set the punchneedle at No 5 and where indicated on the pattern embroider four or five stitches in a circle.

Very pale mauve spikes

These are worked in crewel wool, very pale mauve 891.

Set the punchneedle at No 2 and work in the direction of the arrow shown on the pattern. Change the needle tip to No 1 and work outward alongside the first row to about three stitches from the end of the spike.

Tiny pale mauve flowers

These are worked in crewel wool, pale mauve 101.

There are five tiny flowers. Set the punchneedle at No 2 and work 10 stitches in a circle.

Tiny very dark purple flowers

These are worked in crewel wool, very dark purple, 106.

There are five tiny flowers. Set the punchneedle at No 2 and work 10 stitches in a circle.

Pale green circles

These are worked in crewel wool, pale green 352.

Set the punchneedle at No 6 and embroider 10 stitches in a circle.

Mid green circles

These are worked in crewel wool, mid green 354.

Set the punchneedle at No 6 and embroider 10 stitches in a circle.

Stems

These are worked in crewel wool, dark green 356.

Set the punchneedle at No 2 and embroider along the lines indicated for the stems.

Very dark green area at top of bow

This is worked in tapestry wool, dark green 357.

Set the punchneedle at No 7 and embroider three rows.

Above the dark green, fill in any open area with crewel wool, mid green 354.

Fill-in dots

Finally, around the outside edge and in some places in the centre of the completed design, small dots (loops) are embroidered. They are worked with crewel wool, pale green 352. Set the punchneedle at No 3. The stitches on the back are made longer than in normal stitching, which in turn will give a shorter, more widely spaced loop on the front. These loops are worked at random in areas shown on the pattern. Add more or less dots as required to give an over all balance to the finished design, (see Figure 9b).

Finishing

Trim any long threads on the back. Remove the fabric from the hoop. Stretch the fabric in all directions to straighten the weave.

Press carefully around the embroidery using heat appropriate for woollen fabric.

Make a bow from pale, mid and dark mauve tapestry wool plus the mauve and green organza ribbon. Stitch the bow into place.

Place a layer of pellon under the embroidery prior to making it up into a hot water bottle cover (see special instruction box for Making up Mobile Phone Carrier) or framing it in a pretty frame.

BEAUTIFUL BROOCHES

Skilfully toned hand-dyed silk ribbons add glamour and appeal to these beautiful brooches. They are gorgeous and will be an ideal gift to make for special friends.

Materials

Dancing Ribbon needle

medium punchneedle

20 cm (8 in) lip-lock hoop (if you embroider the three
flowers at one time) or a 15 cm (6 in) lip-lock hoop

30 cm or 25 cm (12 in or 9 in) fabric square

Rajmahal Art silk, colour 44 (Tangier sand) and 115
(Imperial purple)

Kakoonda silk ribbon, 7 mm, 3.5 m (137 in), in mauve
3c and pink 15

13 mm (½ in) bias-cut silk ribbon, 3.5 m (137 in), in
variegated purple with yellow

water-erasable pen

small metal ruler

You Can Wash It craft glue

sewing needle and thread

crochet hook

stamens (optional)—four for each brooch

12 cm (5 in) square of fabric to make up the back of
each brooch

brooch pins/clasps

two cardboard circles 4.5 cm (1 ¾ in) for each brooch.

Preparation

Before starting these brooches, read the information in the box on the Dancing Ribbon needle.

Trace the central circle from the pattern onto
the back of the fabric. Place the fabric very, very
tightly in the hoop.

Embroidery

It is interesting to see from the photograph that
although the same pattern has been used for the
three brooches, the flower brooch embroidered
with 13 mm variegated purple/yellow silk ribbon
looks strikingly different.

TIP

Be aware that the 13 mm bias-cut silk ribbon, because
of its width, does not flow as readily through the needle. This is particularly so if the colours are concentrated
and dark, such as purples and reds. The dye makes the
ribbon harsh. It is particularly necessary to use a very
good quality fabric, along with the twisting motion of
the Dancing Ribbon needle when using this ribbon, and
to take time to practise with it. The results are stunning
and well worth the effort. When using this ribbon, hold
each loop made in place on the front, and as well,
when the needle is withdrawn to the surface after making each loop, draw the needle along the ribbon about
2–3 mm (approx ⅛ in) before moving along to the next
stitch. The short distance the needle is pulled along the
ribbon enables the needle to be more easily positioned
for the next stitch insertion.

Centres

Thread the medium needle with the Rajmahal
silk. When the needle is threaded, tie a knot in
the end of the thread. Read the notes on
Rajmahal art silks in Chapter 2 Requirements.

Set the punchneedle at No 7 and work 20
stitches in a circle (see Stitch Glossary, Figure 5).
With the water-erasable pen, mark the beginning
for the next round. Set the punchneedle at No 6
and work all the way around the former circle.

Continue working in this manner by altering
the length of the needle tip to No 5, work all the
way around, then No 4, work all the way around,
and then No 3. Finally, set the punchneedle at
No 2 and work two rounds.

TIP

Ideally, make the centre at least 2.5 cm (1 in) in
diameter (measured on the back), otherwise the ribbon
loops can cover the centre, leaving very little to be
seen. Further rounds can be made if necessary to bring
the centre up to the required size.

Silk ribbon petals

Note Use the diagrams in the pattern as a guide
only (the instructions actually state how far apart
to embroider each row).

When the centre has been embroidered, mark
the circle for the first round of ribbon onto the

fabric. Embroider that round and then mark out for the next round and so on. The measurements will alter with the various widths of ribbons chosen, so use the design as a guide, mark the fabric and work from those markings.

First round Measure and mark a circle 2 mm (⅛ in) outside the finished centre. On this circle put in 16 marks as indicated on the pattern.

Change to the Dancing Ribbon needle.

Measure the needle tip to 45 mm (1 ¾ in). Thread the chosen silk ribbon, and tie a knot at the end.

With a gentle twisting motion, embroider 16 loops.

TIPS

1 It is not necessary to cut the ribbon at the end of each round. Simply pull the needle gently along the ribbon, set the new needle length and then pull the ribbon from the handle to tighten the ribbon again before beginning the next round. Before beginning the next round, check on the front to see that the last loop of the previous row has not been shortened while the needle tip was being altered.

2 Gently open the ribbon loops as each round is completed.

3 Remember to hold the loops on the front, gently out of the way, as more loops are formed.

Second round With the needle tip measured to 55 mm (approximately 2 ⅛ in), measure 2 mm (⅛ in) away from the first round and embroider 20 stitches around.

Third round With the needle tip measured to 65 mm (just over 2 ½ in), work 2 mm (⅛ in) away from the second round and embroider 20 stitches around.

Finishing

The end tags of silk ribbon have a habit of finding their way through to the front of the work.

To prevent this happening, trim the ends of the ribbon on the back of the piece and fix in place with a tiny amount of You Can Wash It craft glue, which dries clear and soft.

To put the stamens in place, find the knot at the very beginning of the centre of the brooch and remove about five stitches. Push the crochet hook through the fabric at this point and make a 'largish' hole without damaging the fabric. Fold the stamens in half (the stamens that I use have a small bead of colour on each end) and push the fold through the hole from the front to the back. Securely stitch the stamens in place on the back.

Sparingly smear the completed embroidery on the back with You Can Wash It craft glue.

Assembling the brooch

Cut the circle on which the brooch has been embroidered away from the fabric on the mark indicated on the pattern.

With an embroidery needle and a strong thread, doubled, stitch a round of running stitches about 6 mm (¼ in) in from the edge.

Place a cardboard circle cut the size indicated on the pattern onto the back of the brooch and tightly pull up the running stitches. Tie off the stitching securely.

Cut a circle of fabric for covering the backing cardboard the size shown on the pattern. Cover the second cardboard circle with this circle of fabric in the same manner as above.

Position the brooch pin/clasp in place on the fabric-covered side of the second circle and stitch in place. (If your chosen brooch pin does not have holes to stitch through, then glue it into place and set aside to dry.)

Place the two circles back to back and stitch the edges together.

Your beautiful brooch is now ready to wear or to give as a gift to a special friend.

Tracing and construction guide

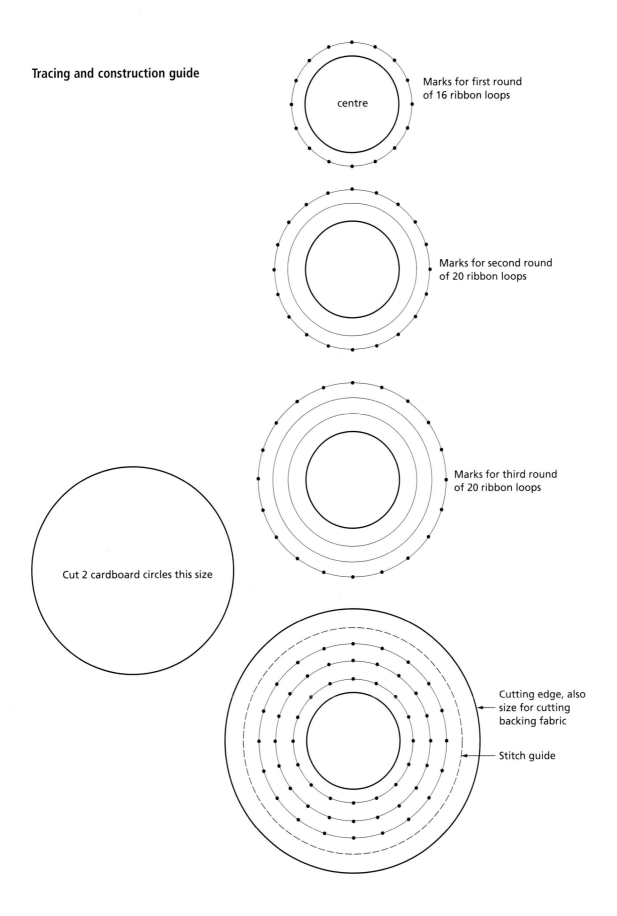

Marks for first round of 16 ribbon loops

centre

Marks for second round of 20 ribbon loops

Marks for third round of 20 ribbon loops

Cut 2 cardboard circles this size

Cutting edge, also size for cutting backing fabric

Stitch guide

THE DANCING RIBBON NEEDLE

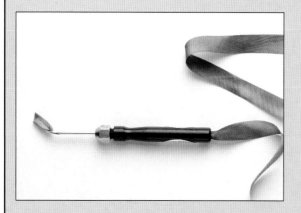

The results achieved when embroidering with the Dancing Ribbon Needle are exquisite. The Dancing Ribbon needle is a punchneedle through which sumptuous silk ribbons, yarns and exotic threads can be used. It is used a little differently to the smaller types of punchneedle to minimise potential damage to the fabric caused by punching the much larger diameter of the ribbon needle and the greater width of ribbon through the fabric.

Any ribbon, thread or yarn can be embroidered with the Dancing Ribbon needle, providing that when it is threaded the ribbon can be gently and easily pulled backwards and forwards through the bore and eye of the needle.

Safety Tips

Owing to its larger size and sharpness, the Dancing Ribbon needle needs to be used with great care. It is necessary to store the sharp needle tip safely when not in use. When purchased, the sharp needle tip is housed inside the handle of the punchneedle for safety. It is recommended that when the Dancing Ribbon needle is not in use you always replace the needle tip in the handle and securely tighten the nut. Care is also needed when working with the Dancing Ribbon needle, as the sharp tip extends quite some distance through the fabric.

To remove the needle from the handle, hold the protruding blunt end, loosen the nut a few turns and fully remove the needle. Reverse the needle, carefully push the blunt end into the handle with the sharp tip protruding and tighten the nut to finger-tight at the needle length required.

Threading the Dancing Ribbon needle

Insert the threader through the eye of the needle. Angle the threader, guide it into the bore of the needle and out through the handle. Thread the ribbon through the threader, and then slip the ribbon up into the small twist at the end of the threader where it will be held securely during threading. Leave only a small tag of ribbon. Gently pull the threader with the ribbon attached all the way through the handle and out through the eye of the needle.

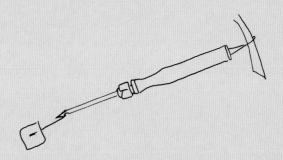

Changing the length of the needle

Different sized loops can be made by changing the length of the needle. Simply loosen the nut, measure the required needle length as indicated in the design, then tighten the nut securely with your fingers.

Measuring the needle

With the Dancing Ribbon needle the loop length is adjusted by measuring from the needle tip to the brass nut. A ruler with no spare on the end is ideal when measuring lengths for this needle (see Ruler in Chapter 2 Requirements).

Using the Dancing Ribbon needle

The ribbons being worked with the Dancing Ribbon needle are wider than normal embroidery threads, so the embroidery method is a little different to that of a regular punchneedle. Also, because of the thickness of the needle and the width of the ribbon being used, there is a risk of damaging some fabrics unless the following method is used.

The fabric needs to be stretched tight in the hoop. Place the needle tip at the point of insertion and guide it through the fabric with a gentle twisting action. This allows the tip to find its way between the fibres, causing very little damage. The action is not like the punch-punch-punch of regular punchneedle embroidery. Twist the needle through the fibres of the fabric, push the needle down to its full length, lift the needle to the surface of the fabric and then slide the needle tip along the fabric to the place where it will be inserted for the next stitch.

Where a flower is being embroidered and the hoop is being turned, the motion becomes twist-push-turn the hoop, pivoting it on the needle, then lifting the needle to the surface again in preparation for the next stitch. As the needle is being withdrawn from the fabric, gently hold the ribbon loop made on the front out of the way, so that with the next insertion of the needle the ribbon is not punched into and therefore damaged.

The tighter the fabric is in the hoop, the easier it is for the needle tip to find its way between the fibres. Once you have practised this form of embroidery fabulous results are possible. If fabric damage does occur, it may be that you will have to use a different fabric or fix an iron-on woven interfacing to the back of the fabric.

Handy Hints

◆ Hold the angled edge of the needle tip facing to the left if you are right-handed, and facing to the right if you are left-handed.

◆ Work from the back of the fabric, gently twisting the length of the needle through the fabric fully up to the handle. There is less chance of punching through loops already worked if the needle tip is angled slightly away from them.

◆ If there is too much resistance when using a particular ribbon or yarn, do not persist. Check the tightness of the fabric in the hoop or try a slightly narrower ribbon.

◆ When starting to embroider, hold the end tag of the ribbon on the back of the fabric to prevent it 'popping' through to the front of the fabric. Alternatively, tie a small knot at the very end of the ribbon to prevent it 'escaping'.

◆ Hold onto the ribbon loops made on the front as the needle tip is withdrawn from the fabric. If the ribbon is not held, the last loop may not stay in place. Holding the previously worked loops out of the way also prevents the Dancing Ribbon needle puncturing and damaging them. Work safely. Mind your fingers when you punch through again.

◆ There may be times when the loop on the front ends up with the ribbon doubled, not open to its full width. With your fingers, gently pull on each side of the loop to help it fully open. Some ribbons fold in half as they are pulled through the needle.

◆ Short loops are not so easy to open. If a loop isn't sitting well, the remedy may be as simple as turning the whole loop inside out to allow it to open out more fully.

◆ To end, hold the ribbon in place with your index finger at the point of exit, then slide the punchneedle along the ribbon a little way before cutting and leaving a small tag.

PRETTY PINK BLOOMS

This striking bouquet of silk ribbon flowers embroidered with the Dancing Ribbon needle will brighten up a corner of any room when mounted in a delicate gold frame.

Materials

Dancing Ribbon needle

medium punchneedle

13 mm (½ in) Kakoonda silk ribbon, variegated pinky-apricot 6F

7 mm (just over ¼ in) Kakoonda silk ribbon, green 306

Rajmahal art silk: Woodlands 171 and Green Earth 421 (see Rajmahal Art Silks in Chapter 2 Requirements)

25 cm (10 in) square of fabric

iron-on woven interfacing (optional)

20 cm (8 in) lip-lock hoop

terracotta half-pot, 4 cm across at top x 4 cm deep (approx 1 ⅝ in x 1 ⅝ in)

small metal ruler

water-erasable pen

You Can Wash It craft glue

Preparation

It is important to consider the type of fabric which has been selected when using the Dancing Ribbon Needle. If the use of interfacing is necessary, iron it onto the back of the fabric.

Mark the design onto the back of the fabric, along with the placement for the pot.

It is necessary to transfer the base line and the grass tufts onto the front of the fabric as well. These will be embroidered in reverse punchneedle embroidery. Mark on the front of the fabric the base line and the grass tufts, which will be embroidered in reverse punchneedle embroidery (see Stitch Glossary, Figure 3b).

Assemble the fabric in the hoop and tighten firmly.

Tracing guide

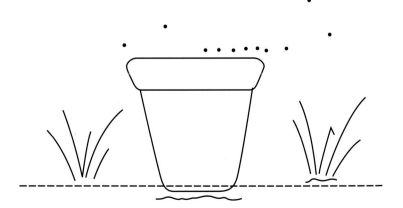

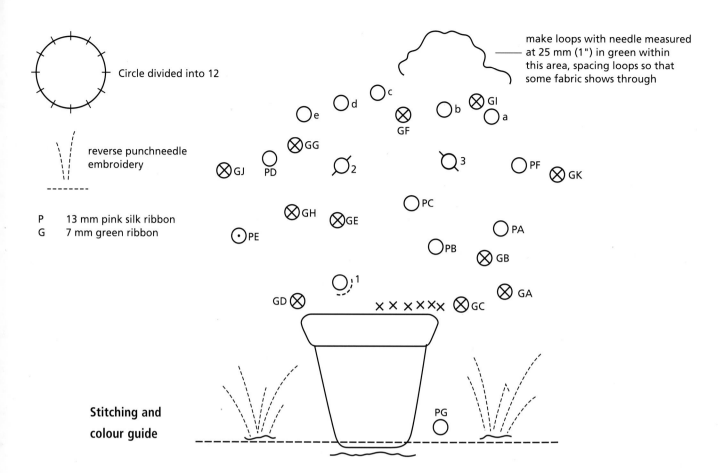

Circle divided into 12

reverse punchneedle embroidery

P   13 mm pink silk ribbon
G   7 mm green ribbon

make loops with needle measured at 25 mm (1") in green within this area, spacing loops so that some fabric shows through

Stitching and colour guide

Embroidery

No 1 Flower

The centre Use the medium punchneedle and six strands of Rajmahal Woodlands to work the centre in a circle (see Stitch Glossary, Figure 5).

Set the punchneedle at No 7. Work 12 stitches in a circle.

Set the punchneedle at No 6, mark the start, and work all the way around the first row.

Set the punchneedle at No 5 and work all the way around the second row.

Set the punchneedle at No 4 and work all the way around.

Ribbon loops With the water-erasable pen, mark four equal quarters around the centre. Now divide each quarter in three with two equally spaced marks. This will give 12 markings where each loop will be worked (see diagram above).

Change to the Dancing Ribbon needle.

Measure the needle tip (see box, The Dancing Ribbon Needle, in Beautiful Brooches) to 45 mm (1 ⅞ in).

Thread the needle with the 13 mm variegated pinky-apricot ribbon.

Gently work 12 stitches all the way around the centre, one loop on each mark on the fabric.

If a rounded, convex-topped terracotta pot has been chosen, the three or four loops at the bottom edge of this flower, marked on the pattern with a curved line of dashes, might need to be worked with the length of the needle tip altered to 50 mm (2 in) to give sufficient length to allow the ribbon loops to spill over the top of the pot.

Turn the piece over to gently open the ribbon loops.

TIP

After the ribbon loops have been pulled open with the fingers, to further unfurl them, use the rounded handle of a crochet hook (take care to keep the hook away from the ribbon) or a knitting needle. Roll the roundness of the needle inside the ribbon loops, which assists in opening the loops out fully.

No 2 Flower

The centre Use the medium punchneedle and six strands of Rajmahal Woodlands to work the centre in a circle.

Set the punchneedle at No 4 and work 12 stitches in a circle.

Set the punchneedle at No 3, mark the start, and work all the way around the first row

Set the punchneedle at No 2 and work all the way around the second row

Set the punchneedle at No 1 and work all the way around.

Ribbon loops With the water-erasable pen, mark four equal quarters around the centre. Now divide each quarter in three with two equally spaced marks. This will give 12 markings where each loop will be worked.

Change to the Dancing Ribbon needle.

Thread the needle with the 13 mm variegated pinky-apricot ribbon.

Measure the needle tip to 35 mm (1 ⅜ in).

With this flower, work six stitches above the line marked on the pattern.

When the six loops have been worked, hold the ribbon in place at the exit point of the last stitch punched into place. Withdraw the ribbon needle. Gently pull the needle about 15 cm (6 in) along the ribbon.

Change the needle tip to 45 cm (1 ⅞ in) to work the remaining six stitches below the line. Tighten the ribbon in preparation to begin placing further loops by pulling it from where it emerges from the handle. Before starting to punch with the longer loop, turn the work to the front to check that the last loop worked has not been pulled shorter when altering the needle length.

Turn the piece over to gently open the ribbon loops.

No 3 Flower

Centre Work the same as No 2 flower.

Ribbon loops Change to the Dancing Ribbon Needle.

Work similarly to No 2 flower, except that you work only five loops (not six) above the marked line, at 35 mm (1 ⅜ in). Work the remaining seven loops at 45 mm (1 ⅞ in).

Gently open the ribbon loops.

Remaining flowers

The seven remaining full flowers, PA to PG, and the five bud flowers, a to e, are each marked on the pattern with a circle. They are worked in the pinky-apricot silk ribbon. Each circle has, for example, PA (the P indicating pink ribbon) or a, b, c, etc next to it.

Full flowers See list below and work each flower as indicated. The instructions are written, for example, 45 mm (1 ⅞ in), 7. This means that the needle tip is set at 45 mm and seven loops are worked.

PA – 45 mm (1 ⅞ in), 7
PB – 40 mm (1 ⅝ in), 6
PC – 35 mm (1 ⅜ in), 5
PD – 35 mm (1 ⅜ in), 6
PE – 40 mm (1 ⅝ in), 7
PF – 40 mm (1 ⅝ in), 7
PG – 35 mm (1 ⅜ in), 3

Bud flowers When the needle tip is at a short length such as 35 mm (1 ⅜ in), there is not sufficient length of ribbon emerging on the front to open out. The unfurled loops look more bud-like when embroidered at this length.

a – 25 mm (1 in), 3
b – 25 mm (1 in), 5
c – 25 mm (1 in), 5
d – 25 mm (1 in), 5
e – 30 mm (1 ⅛ in), 5

Greenery among the flowers

The 11 areas among the flowers worked in 7 mm green silk ribbon, GA to GK, are marked on the pattern with an X. Each X has, for example, GA (the G indicating green ribbon) next to it. The notation is the same as for the flowers.

GA – 35 mm (1 ⅜ in), 5
GB – 35 mm (1 ⅜ in), 5
GC – 60 mm (2 ⅜ in), 7
GD – 60 mm (2 ⅜ in), 7
GE – 55 mm (2 ⅛ in), 5
GF – 35 mm (1 ⅜ in), 5
GG – 30 mm (1 ⅛ in), 5
GH – 35 mm (1 ⅜ in), 5
GI – 30 mm (1 ⅛ in), 2
GJ – 35 mm (1 ⅜ in), 5
GK – 35 mm (1 ⅜ in), 5

Greenery at top of pot There are six Xs marked along the top of the pot. Set the needle tip at 50 mm (2 in) and make six loops in a row with the green ribbon.

Greenery above flowers The flowers are enhanced with a small area marked at the top of the blooms where green loops are made with the needle tip measured at 25 mm (1 in). Space the loops so that some of the background fabric shows through. Be guided by the colour photograph.

Greenery surrounding terracotta pot

All this greenery is worked with six strands of Rajmahal green thread. On the pattern its position is marked with lines of dashes. Work these in reverse punchneedle embroidery (see Stitch Glossary, Figure 3b).

Wavy lines Set the punchneedle at No 2. The wavy line immediately under the pot is worked from the back giving loops on the front.

The two areas marked with wavy lines immediately under the spiky greenery are worked from the back with the needle set at No 12 giving loops on the front. These loops are cut open to give the grassy tufty look.

Grass tufts Now set the punchneedle at No 2 and work a row of reverse punchneedle embroidery from the front over the bottom of the cut loops, as shown in the diagram. This reverse punchneedle embroidery will hold the long loops upright.

When long loops have been cut, they tend to angle outwards. Working reverse punchneedle embroidery over the base of the cut loops holds them upright. When this stitching is finished, carefully cut the tufts unevenly to give a more realistic grassy appearance.

Fallen flower

Near the pot, on the base line, punch three loops of pinky-apricot ribbon with the Dancing Ribbon needle measured to 35 mm (1 ⅜ in).

Finishing

Remove the work from the hoop. Stretch the fabric in all directions. Carefully press around the outside of the embroidery.

If a shiny look is desired for the terracotta pot, paint over it with a glaze and leave to dry. Carefully glue the terracotta pot into place, pushing it up under the ribbon loops so that they flow over the top of the pot. Avoid getting any glue on the ribbons. Leave to dry.

To check for balance of the design, turn the finished piece of embroidery upside down to view it from all angles. If it looks unbalanced, replace it in the hoop to embroider some further loops.

Place pellon under the completed piece before framing. Frame appropriately and enjoy your pot of gorgeous pink blooms.

Stitching on the front is worked over the loops

SUPERB SILKS ON SATIN

The lustre of the delicate toned Rajmahal art silks add elegance to this superb silk ribbon embroidery, which is showcased perfectly on a beautiful cream satin cushion.

Materials

large and medium punchneedles

25 cm (10 in) lip-lock embroidery hoop

35 cm (14 in) square of fabric

Rajmahal art silks

4 mm silk ribbons, YLI dark mauve 32 and light
    mauve 33

iron-on woven interfacing (optional)

Threads

Rajmahal Art Silks

  dainty lilac 111

  purple dusk 113

  imperial purple 115

  green earth 421

  wheat gold 91

  Moroccan gold 94

  Tangier sand 44

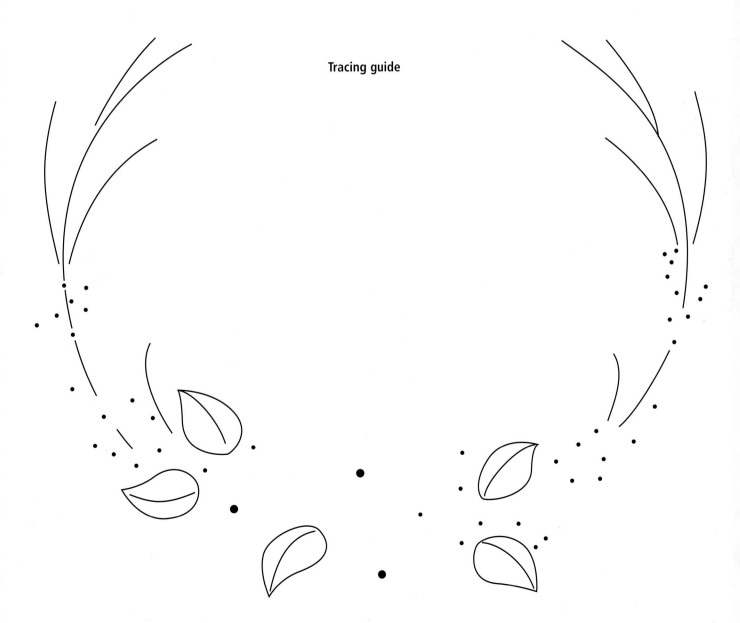

Tracing guide

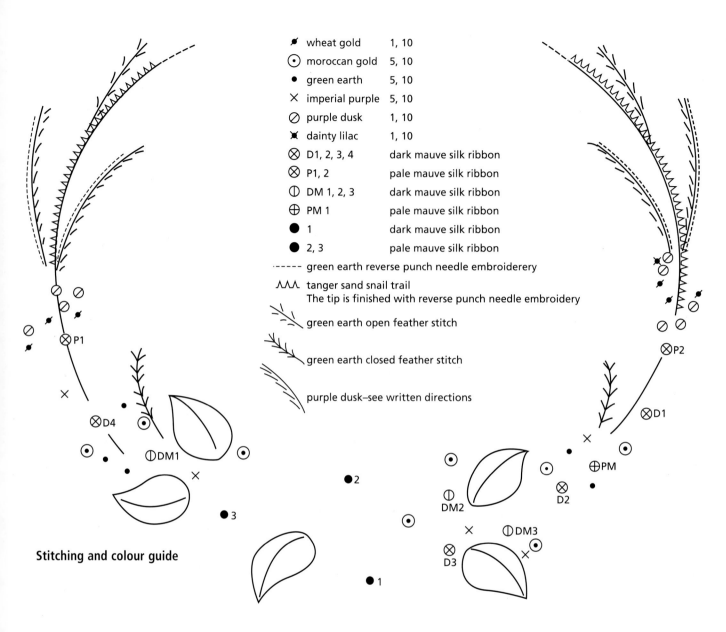

✒	wheat gold	1, 10
⊙	moroccan gold	5, 10
●	green earth	5, 10
✕	imperial purple	5, 10
⊘	purple dusk	1, 10
✱	dainty lilac	1, 10
⊗	D1, 2, 3, 4	dark mauve silk ribbon
⊗	P1, 2	pale mauve silk ribbon
⦶	DM 1, 2, 3	dark mauve silk ribbon
⊕	PM 1	pale mauve silk ribbon
●	1	dark mauve silk ribbon
●	2, 3	pale mauve silk ribbon

- - - - - green earth reverse punch needle embroiderery

ʌʌʌ tanger sand snail trail
The tip is finished with reverse punch needle embroidery

green earth open feather stitch

green earth closed feather stitch

purple dusk–see written directions

Stitching and colour guide

Preparation

If necessary iron the woven interfacing onto the back of the fabric.

Trace the design on to the back of the fabric.

Place the fabric in the hoop with the traced design uppermost. Ensure that the fabric is extremely taut in the hoop

The leaves and some areas of green are embroidered from the front. Lightly trace these onto the front of the fabric in preparation for the embroidery. As well, trace the longest line for the semi-circle onto the front as this is worked from the front with open snail trail (see Special Effects, sample g, p54).

The medium punchneedle is used with six strands of Rajmahal thread

The large punchneedle is used for the 4 mm silk ribbon.

Follow the legend on the Stitching and Colour Guide for the placement of colours and stitches used.

See Working with Silk Ribbon in Chapter 3 Techniques.

No 1 Flower

Centre Use the medium punchneedle set at No 3. Working with the Rajmahal Imperial purple 115, embroider 20 stitches in a circle (see Stitch Glossary, Figure 5).

Mark the end of the first round of the circle to indicate the start of the second round.

Change to No 2 and work all the way around the initial circle.

Flower petals These are embroidered with silk ribbon.

With the water erasable pen, mark 16 points on the circle (see diagram 1).

Set the needle at No 12. Tie a knot in the dark mauve silk ribbon where it is pulled though the eye of the needle. The knot prevents the end tag from working its way through to the front of the fabric. Embroider 16 loops around the embroidered centre.

Cut the silk ribbon. Keep the needle threaded. Remove the casing and spring from the punchneedle, which exposes the full length of the tip (approx. 50 mm / 2 in from the tip to the handle), and store safely (see Long Loops in Chapter 2 Requirements). The needle will still be threaded when removed from the casing.

Tie a knot in the silk ribbon.

Mark 20 dots for the outer circle of loops, 2 mm away from the previous row (see diagrams 2 and 3).

Punch the full length of the needle, right up to the hilt, to form extra long loops for the outside row of petals. Hold the ribbon loops out of the way on the underside to prevent the needle tip from punching through the loops already made Continue until all the large petals are created. Hold the ribbon in place at the point of exit of the needle in the fabric and cut.

Flowers No 2 and 3

These are worked the same as flower No 1, except that the centres are embroidered with Rajmahal purple dusk 113, and the pale mauve silk ribbon is used for the petals.

Flowers D1, D2, D3, D4

Centres Using the medium punchneedle set at No 3, work 20 stitches in a circle (see stitch glossary). The centre of D1 is embroidered in Rajmahal dainty lilac 111; D2, Rajmahal purple dusk 113; D3 and D4, Rajmahal imperial purple 115.

Petals With the water-erasable pen, mark 16 points around the circle (see diagram 1).

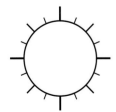

Diagram 1
1. Mark circle into quarters
2. Mark between the quarters to make 8 points
3. Mark betwen the eighths to make 16 points.

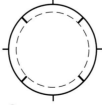

Diagram 2
1. Mark circle 2 mm outside finished first row of silk ribbon loops
2. Make a mark inwards to divide the circle into quarters. This mark is a guide only.

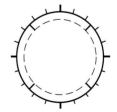

Diagram 3
On either side of the inwards mark put in 2 marks. This gives 20 points for the embroidery.

Marking for 4mm silk ribbon flowers. Note: Use the diagram as a guide only (the instruction actually states how to embroider each row).

Set the needle at No 12. Tie a knot in the dark mauve silk ribbon and embroider 16 loops around the embroidered centre of the four flowers.

Flowers P1 and P2

These are worked the same as the D flowers above, except that the centres are in Rajmahal purple dusk 113 and the petals in pale mauve silk ribbon.

Flowers DM1, DM2, DM3

These three flowers are embroidered with dark mauve silk ribbon. Set the punchneedle at No 8 and work 12 stitches in a circle.

Flower PM

This flower is worked in pale mauve silk ribbon. Set the punchneedle at No 8 and work 12 stitches in a circle.

Small filler flowers

To complete the remaining small flowers indicated by various symbols on the pattern, embroidered in various Rajmahal colours, follow the pattern for the placement of colours and how many stitches to use.

Use whatever colour and length of loop is indicated on the pattern for each individual flower. Where the pattern indicates, for example, 1, 10, this means to set the needle at No 1 and work 10 stitches around in a circle. Commence each circle by punching directly into the centre of each symbol and then work the circle with the required number of stitches.

Large leaves

Set the needle at No 3 to begin. Follow the method for embroidering a leaf in the Stitch Glossary, Figure 8.

Feathery stalks

For the remainder of the design, follow the pattern and refer to the Stitch Glossary to complete the embroidery at the top of the semi-circle.

On the left, the purple dusk 113 stalk is embroidered from the back. Set the punchneedle at No 1. Start at the top. Make four stitches down, then two stitches out to the left but up at a 45-degree angle. Work directly over these two stitches back to the stalk. Make three stitches down and two out and up to the left. Repeat to the end.

On the right, reverse the direction for the flowers on the stalk.

The feathery stalks in green earth are embroidered in open feather stitch (see Special Effects, sample d, p53), and the stalks in tangier sand in snail trail (see Special Effects, sample f, p54).

Finishing

Remove the fabric from the hoop and stretch in all directions to straighten out the grain of the fabric.

Carefully press around the embroidery.

This delightful silk ribbon design can be made into a cushion or framed in a box frame. If making into a cushion, stitch borders around the fabric square on which the embroidery has been worked. Make a cord (see Cord Making in Chapter 3 Techniques) with the various Rajmahal colours and stitch it around the square of embroidery.

LEESA'S BAG

This fan-shaped bag has been teamed with the oriental look of cherry blossoms, which are embroidered simply and easily in punch needle embroidery. The wonderful technique of blending threads to make subtle changes of colour works superbly well for the blossoms.

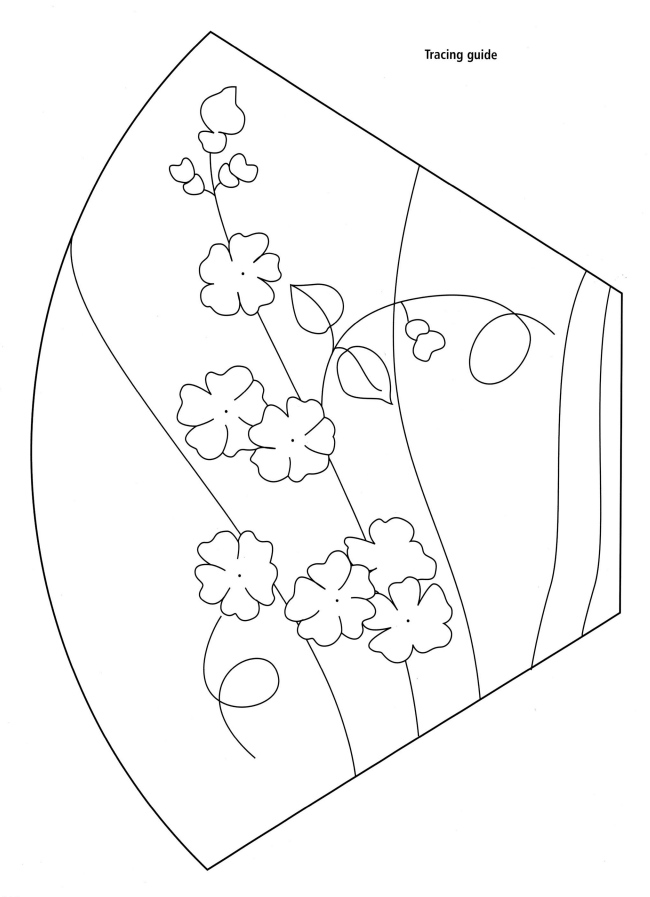

Tracing guide

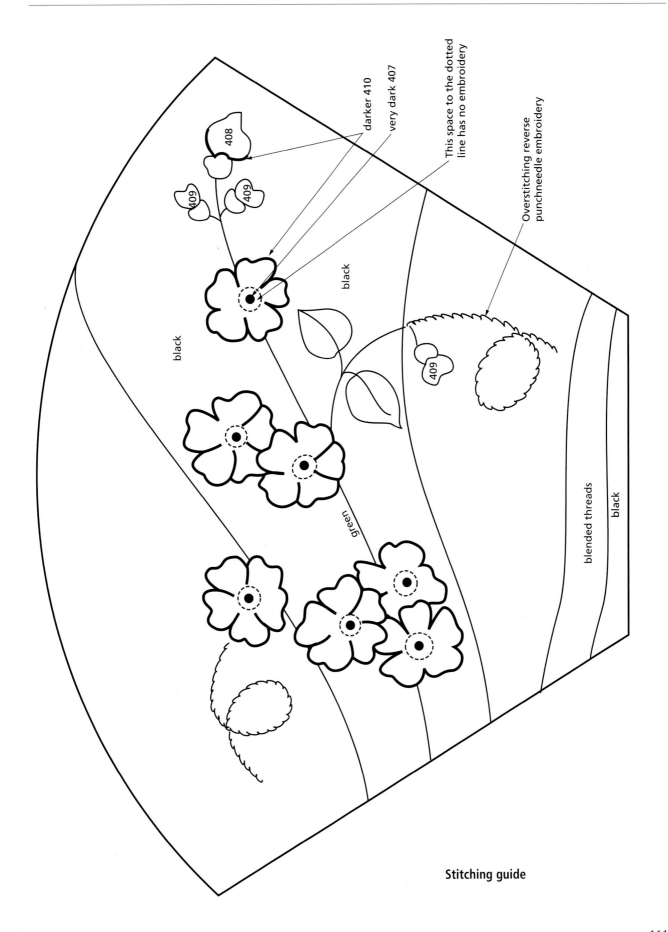

Stitching guide

Materials

small and medium punch needles

25 cm (10 in) lip-lock hoop

35 cm (14 in) square of tightly woven fabric
for the embroidery plus extra for making
up the bag

lining fabric for the bag

sharp embroidery scissors

You Can Wash It craft glue

iron-on transfer pen (see note)

You Can Wash It craft glue

fine steel crochet hook

pellon

spray glue for assembling the bag

cardboard for making up the bag

purchased handle

Threads

	Madeira	DMC
very dark pink	407	347
pale pink	408	3328
mid pink	409	3706
darker pink	410	3705
dark pink	412	892
green	1612	732
black 2-ply acrylic yarn		
black	2400	310

(optional if black 2-ply acrylic yarn is not available)

Preparation

If a dark fabric is chosen it can be difficult to see a design traced onto it. There are various ways that this can be done (see Transferring a Design in Chapter 3 Techniques).

Embroidery

Flowers

Centres Use six strands of very dark pink 407 in the medium punch needle. Set the punch needle at No 1. Work 10 stitches in a circle (see Stitch Glossary, Figure 5).

Petals Use three strands of thread through the small punch needle. Set the punch needle at No 1.

The petals are embroidered in the blending technique (see Stitch Glossary, Figure 13) Commence stitching from the outside edge, changing and blending the colours as shown in the diagram.

3D	2D 1M	2M 1D	3M	3M 1L	2L 1M	3L

Blending 3 strands of thread with
3 colours for the flowers
D = 410
M = 409
L = 408

The first colour used, the dark pink, is worked all around the outline shown on the pattern; begin to blend in the medium pink and then begin to blend in the light pink.

There will be a small space in the centre of each flower where there are no stitches. This allows the background fabric to show through. If the background fabric is dark as in this project, the colour showing through gives added effect. If this is not pleasing, depending on the choice of fabric then extend the last colour change of the blending to meet the dark pink centre into the centre.

Leaves

The leaves and calyx are embroidered with three strands of green. The vein of each leaf is made in black.

Stem

The main stem within the black area is made with the medium punch needle and six strands of green. The stems outside the black area are embroidered with three strands of green in overstitching reverse punch needle embroidery (see Special Effects, sample e, p53).

Buds

Use three strands of thread and follow the colours indicated on the pattern for the four buds.

Black area behind flowers

Fill in the whole area with the black 2-ply acrylic yarn and set the punch needle at No 1.

Blending for the base

Embroider the black area first.

Next to the last row of black commence shading and blending with three strands of thread. However, four colours, not three as used in the flowers, are used in the blending here. Commence with two rows of the very dark pink. Follow the chart for the blending process for this area.

The first 2 rows are worked with 3 strands of the very dark pink.

The next row, 2 strands of the very dark pink with 1 strand of the dark pink.

The next row, 2 strands of dark pink with 1 strand of very dark pink.

Follow this with a row of 3 strands of dark pink.

The next row, 2 strands of dark pink with 1 strand of medium pink.

Next, 2 strands of medium pink and 1 strand of dark pink.

Follow this with a row of 3 strands of medium pink.

Next, 2 strands of medium pink and 1 strand of light pink.

Next row, 2 strands of light pink and 1 strand of medium.

Final row, 3 strands of light pink.

Finishing

Remove the fabric from the hoop and stretch in all directions. Press around the edges of the embroidery with an iron.

Making up the bag

All piecing requires a 6 mm (¼ in) seam allowance unless otherwise stated.

Front and back panels

Using the large pattern piece (diagram 1), cut out two fan shapes, adding a 12 mm (½ in) seam allowance all round. One of these fan shapes will have the embroidery worked on it.

Side and base strip

Using the patterns (diagrams 2 and 3), cut one base piece and two side pieces from cardboard. Cut out the Vs as well. Use these pieces as templates, placing them end to end on bag fabric, with the base in the middle. Draw around them in one long strip and add 6 mm (¼ in) seam allowance. Do not cut out the V at the ends of the fabric.

Use this fabric strip as a pattern for cutting out a strip of lining and a strip of pellon as well.

Place lining and bag strips, right sides together, then add the pellon strip on one side of the 'sandwich'.

Sew around all sides, leaving an opening in the

3VD (2rows)	2VD 1D	2D 1VD	3D	2D 1M	2M 1D	3M	2M 1L	2L 1M	3L

Blending 3 strands of thread using four different colours
VD = very dark pink 407
D = dark pink 410
M = medium pink 409
L = light pink 408

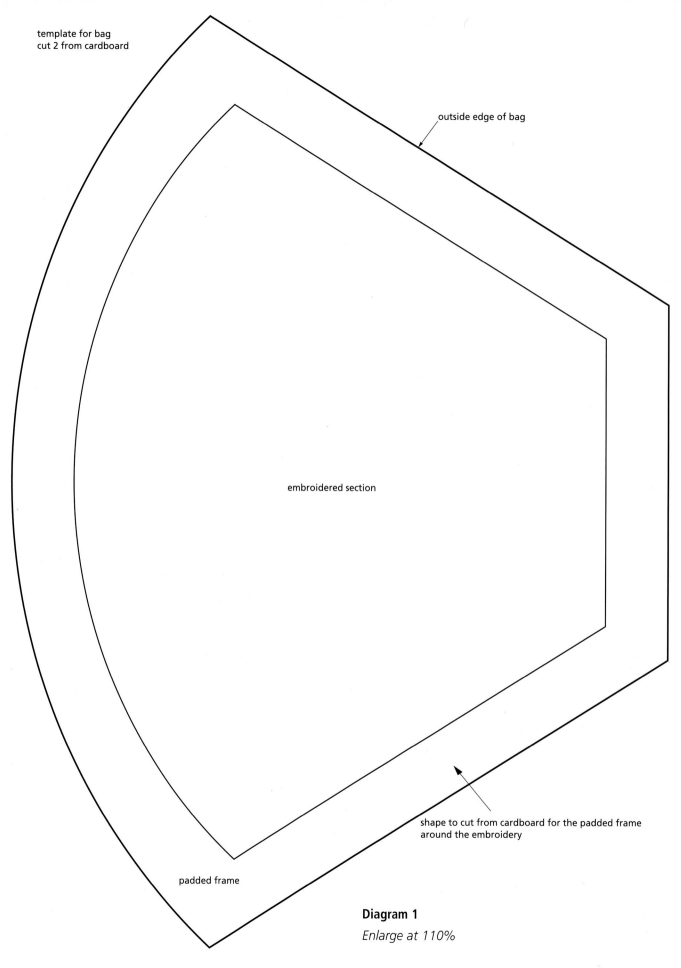

template for bag
cut 2 from cardboard

outside edge of bag

embroidered section

shape to cut from cardboard for the padded frame
around the embroidery

padded frame

Diagram 1
Enlarge at 110%

Diagram 2—Bag base cut from cardboard

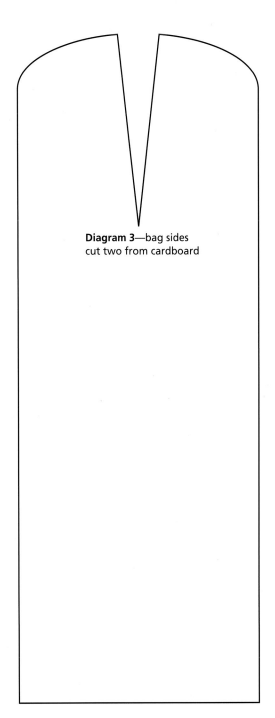

Diagram 3—bag sides
cut two from cardboard

middle on one long side. Turn right sides out and press. Insert the side-panel cardboard pieces into each end of the strip and sew across the strip flush with the cardboard to hold it in place. Then insert the base piece of cardboard and slip-stitch the opening closed.

Lining

From lining fabric cut two fan shapes using the main bag template and add 12 mm (½ in) seam allowance around all sides.

Handles

Use purchased handles as shown on the photograph.

Cut a strip of fabric 5 x 30 cm (2 x 12 in). Fold in half lengthways and press. Press both raw edges in to meet centre fold. Stitch close to the edge on both sides. Cut the strip in four and insert into slits/loops of handle. Stitch onto seam allowance of lining panel before sewing lining and outer bag pieces together. Make sure that the loops are all the same distance from the top of the bag.

Bag construction

Create a cardboard template from bag panel template. Use this to cut four fan shapes from the cardboard (two for outer and two for lining).

Spray-glue all card pieces and place onto a piece of pellon. Let dry and cut out.

Stretch the four fan-shaped fabric pieces (bag fabric and lining) over the card shapes, pellon side to wrong side of fabric. Using a paper glue stick, glue seam allowance onto back of cardboard, clipping fabric where required. Take care not to get glue on edges of card. Glue sides first, then top, then base.

Place one bag side and one lining side together, right sides out, and starting at the base of the bag, slip-stitch sides and base strip to front and back of bag, making sure to match the corners at the bottom of the bag by pinning together where required.

Padded shaped frame for outer front edge of bag

Cut the frame shape as shown on the pattern from a piece of thin cardboard. Check that the frame fits comfortably around the embroidered edges. If stretching of the fabric occurred during the embroidery it might be necessary to carefully remove some stitches from the outside rows of the embroidery to make the embroidery fit perfectly into the frame.

Cut a frame-shaped piece of pellon, and glue to the cardboard.

Cut a 30 cm (12 in) square of fabric. Place the fabric square over the top of the pellon-covered cardboard.

Cut around the outside of the frame shape, leaving 15 mm (⅝ in) fabric as a seam allowance.

Clip the rounded top edge of the fabric. Glue the seam allowance onto the cardboard.

Cut out the fabric in the centre of the frame leaving 15 mm (⅝ in) fabric as a seam allowance.

Clip, glue and stretch the fabric into position.

The padded frame can be attached either by stitching or glueing it in place around the embroidered section.

Make a cord (see Stitch Glossary) and glue or stitch into place around the frame.

This beautifully embroidered and functional bag is now completed for your enjoyment.

VIBRANT VELVET DAISIES

Vibrant and velvet, these daisies take on a life of their own when embroidered with 2-ply acrylic yarn, which has the astonishing property that when the punched loops are cut the thread alters to reveal a rich, plush, velvet appearance. These brightly coloured daisies offer an exciting embellishment to a black pashmina, shawl or sweater.

Tracing guide

Colour guide

work gold to the mark

relief cutting

relief cutting

relief cutting

work gold to the mark

cutting edge

Requirements

medium punchneedle

25 cm (10 in) lip-lock hoop

35 cm (14 in) square of black fabric

small, sharp, pointy embroidery scissors

You Can Wash It craft glue

white pen or other appropriate method for
*   transferring the design onto black fabric (see*
*   Techniques)*

Thread
2-ply acrylic yarn

Cameo	Pretty Punch
teal 50	*jade 45*
peacock 75	*peacock 74*
spring green 71	*kelly green 4*
turquoise deep 83	*deep turquoise 53*
green 27	*emerald green 66*
royal blue 12	*royal blue 49*
dark lavender 97	*grape 8 (not exact match)*
magenta 15	*raspberry 6*
turquoise 11	*turquoise 48*
yellow 45	*bright lemon 55*
gold 46	*yellow/gold 56*
black	*black*
deep red 86	*poinsettia red 62*
hot pink 88	*neon 2 (not exact match)*

gold—colour and brand optional, as this is used
only for a highlight on the edge (Au Papillon or
Butterfly Brand gold, Madeira metallic No 5,
colour 5014, or three strands of DMC gold 5284)

TIP

Be mindful that there is a problem where exact colour matches are not available when converting colours from one brand to another. When a design is not embroidered with the exact suggested colours, the compromise colours can 'throw' the overall balance of the finished work.

Embroidery

Refer to Chapter 5 Another Dimension to learn about the shaping technique which has been used for this colourful design.

Centres and petals

Each section of the design is worked from the outside edge in towards the centre.

Begin each row with the needle tip set at No 3.

Cut the loops open after each row is worked.

Fill in the areas by increasing the needle tip by one number for each round until the remainder of the area is filled up. Cut each loop at the end of each round.

There will be some centre areas where the needle tip will be set at No 8 and No 9.

Trim the edges into shape by removing any cut threads which overhang the original line drawn on the design.

Stem

Set the punchneedle at No 3 and work one row on the marked line. Cut the row of loops. On either side of the cut loops punch in a row with the punchneedle set at No 2. Cut each loop and trim the stem to shape.

The pattern indicates places for cutting in the relief in five of the leaves. On this line an indent can be sculpted in relief to give yet another dimension to the shaped leaves. See Cutting in Relief in Chapter 5 Another Dimension.

Edging

Use the medium punchneedle set at No 1. Embroider one row with the loops close together.

The upper section is embroidered in black. The lower section is worked with a gold thread threaded through the needle with the black. Use any gold thread that will flow readily with the black acrylic yarn. The part which is to be worked with gold is indicated on the pattern.

Finishing

Check each section of work to make sure that all of the loops have been cut and the outside edges have been carefully trimmed. A good, strong light is necessary as it is easy to miss cutting some loops.

Glue the outer black and gold edge on the back, taking care that the glue penetrates the fibres of the fabric, which will prevent the fabric from fraying. Leave to dry.

Remove the fabric from the hoop and shake it well to remove filaments of fluff.

Cut closely around the outside edge.

Attach the completed piece to a shawl, pashmina or sweater by either stitching or glueing in place.

PRETTY PANSIES

The much loved pansy adds a decidedly 'Victorian parlour' touch to this delightful footstool. Embroidered with rich-coloured 2-ply acrylic yarn, this dear little stool can be passed down through the family and enjoyed for many years.

Materials

medium punchneedle
25 cm (10 in) lip-lock hoop
40 cm (16 in) square of fabric
sharp embroidery scissors
fine steel crochet hook
iron-on transfer pen
circular padded footstool at appropriate size

Threads

One thickness of Cameo acrylic yarn is used in the medium punchneedle.

bone	*3*
orchid	*4*
navy	*13*
magenta	*15*
wine	*20*
aspen green	*25*
dark aspen	*26*

Tracing guide

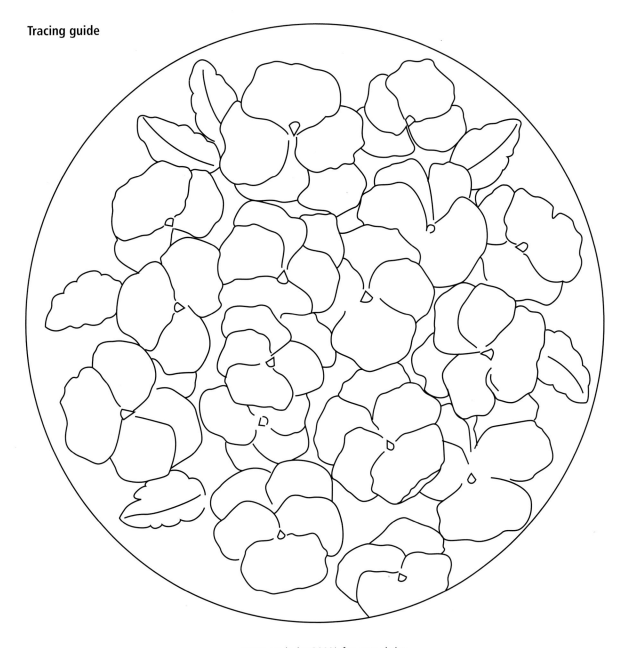

Note: scale by 200% for actual size

Diagram for centres

⋀ 4 or so loops in either green or cream

⋃ yellow

⬙ then punch in 3–4 loops of green in the centre

Colour guide

light rose	31	rust	56
lavender	36	pumpkin	72
purple	37	terracotta	85
brandy	39	grape	87
lemon	42	burgundy	95
baby yellow	43	dark lavender	97
yellow	45	fuchsia	98
antique gold	47		

Preparation

Trace the design onto the back of the fabric.

Place the fabric in the hoop with the traced design uppermost. Ensure that the fabric is extremely tight in the hoop.

Embroidery

The placements for the various colours used in this design are indicated on the colour guide.

Note The circle of pansies is 30 cm (12 in) in diameter and the hoop is 25 cm (10 in) in diameter, so it will be necessary to move the hoop from time to time and to tighten it over previously embroidered areas (see Doughnut Techniques).

Petals

Outline every outside edge area of the petals with the punchneedle set at No 1, with the stitching very close together. Fill in each petal area with the needle tip set at No 2.

Whiskers

The whiskers are worked at No 1 with the stitches very close together.

TIP

Leave a small space around the whiskers as the petal is filled in. This space allows the whiskers to appear as clear lines and prevents the loops of the whiskers and petals becoming intermingled.

Dots

On some petals, for example, flower No 8, dots are indicated on the pattern. Using the threads indicated on the colour guide, work the needle gently through the previously formed loops in a meandering way, (see Stitch Glossary, Figure 9) checking on the front that the dots are showing clearly on the front. If the dots are not showing,

lengthen the needle tip a little bit (see Stitch Glossary, Figure 14).

Centres

See diagram on the pattern. The upside-down V part can be embroidered in either green or cream, alternating the colour. The curve joining them is worked in yellow. When these two parts are finished, embroider three or four loops of green into the centre.

Leaves

Work the veins at No 2 in any colour other than green (this row of stitching will be removed). Work the outside edges of the leaves in dark aspen 26, at No 1, with the stitches very close together. Fill in each area and around the veins at No 2. Leave a small space around the veins as the leaf is filled in. Remove the previously embroidered coloured stitching of the veins and re-work in green with the punchneedle set at No 1 and with the stitches very close together.

TIP

When worked in this manner, the stitching at No 1 gives just a slight definition to the veins in the leaf, in preference to working a different coloured green to make them show up.

Finishing

Remove the fabric from the hoop.

Stretch the fabric in all directions to straighten the embroidery.

Press around the embroidery carefully to remove any marks which may be left by the hoop.

Assembly

Cut around the embroidery leaving at least 5 cm (2 in) of fabric.

With a sewing needle and strong thread, stitch a line of running stitches around the seam

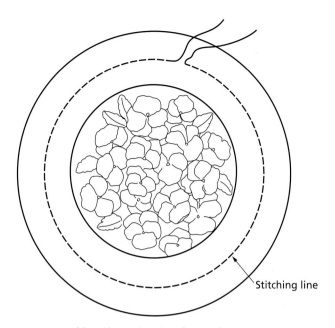

Assembling the embroidery for the footstool.

Cut around shape leaving 5 cm (2") seam allowance.
Work a running stitch along the stitch line.
Leave the thread ends as shown.

allowance as shown in the diagram.

Place a piece of pellon or thin wadding between the embroidery and the padded cover of the footstool.

Centre the fabric over the rounded, padded shape of the footstool. Pull the running stitches tight and pull the embroidery under the round shape. Secure the ends of the sewing thread.

Take a very strong thread and lace the fabric from side to side all the way around the fabric which is pulled under the padded top. Pull very tight. The tighter the fabric the less puckering there will be.

Assemble the wooden base with the feet and the covered round shape.

Take four thickness of the darker green colour used in the embroidery as well as two lengths of gold to make a cord long enough to go around the footstool (see Cord Making, Chapter 3).

Carefully glue the cord into place around the base of the embroidery.

TORTOISE FLOWER POWER

A train of tortoises colourfully parades over a wool cashmere baby capsule cover.
They are simply created in traditional punchneedle embroidery. A variety of threads
can be used, from 2-ply acrylic yarn to crewel wool or stranded cotton.

Materials

*medium punchneedle if using acrylic yarn or
   crewel wool*

*small punchneedle if using 3 strands of
   embroidery cotton*

25 cm (10 in) lip-lock hoop

35 cm (14 in) square of fabric

wool/cashmere baby capsule cover

sharp embroidery scissors

fine steel crochet hook

iron-on transfer pen

Acrylic yarns

Use one thickness of acrylic yarn in the medium
punchneedle.

   Below are colours which can be used from the
acrylic yarn range. These tortoises have been
worked in Cameo yarns. Many of the colours in
the Pretty Punch range have no direct colour
match. I have chosen colours from this range
which will work well together.

Cameo	Pretty Punch
medium green 28	jade 47
radiant blue 74	bright blue 51
wine red 94	cardinal 72
magenta 15	raspberry 6
burnt orange 73	burnt orange 73
black 1	black 58
yellow 45	bright lemon 55
dark lavender 97	grape 7
fuchsia 98	peacock 74
deep pink 77	hot pink 2
brandy 39	burnt orange 39
ocean spray 23	deep turquoise 53
powder blue 7	sky blue 21

Threads

This design can be embroidered with three
strands of embroidery thread in a small
punchneedle.

	DMC	Madeira
green	910	1303
blue	825	1011
red	815	513
orange	608	205
yellow	725	108
purple	550	714
black		
magenta	915	705
sea green	3841	1203

Preparation

Trace the design onto the back of the square of
fabric.

   Place the fabric in the hoop with the traced
design uppermost. Ensure that the fabric is
extremely tight in the hoop.

Embroidery

The tortoises have not been worked directly onto
the baby capsule cover. They have been
embroidered onto the square of fabric, cut out
and then glued into place.

   Follow the placement for the colours in the
colour photograph.

   Embroider the complete outlines of the
tortoises with the loops very, very close together
to achieve an unbroken line.

   Use the medium punchneedle for the acrylic
yarn or the small punchneedle for three strands
of embroidery thread.

   The needle is set at No 1 throughout.

   Embroider the colours as indicated in the
pattern.

Tracing and colour guide

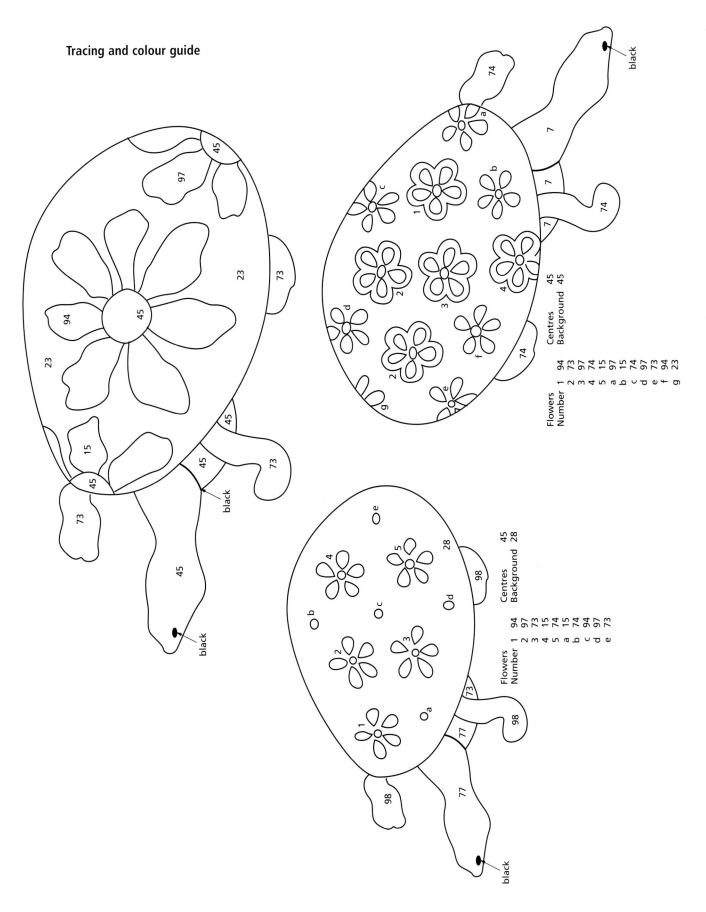

Flowers
Number 1 94
2 73
3 97
4 74
5 15
a 97
b 15
c 74
d 97
e 73
f 94
g 23
Centres 45
Background 45

Flowers
Number 1 94
2 97
3 73
4 15
5 74
a 15
b 74
c 94
d 97
e 73
Centres 45
Background 28

TIP

To get the very best effect for this design, it is important to leave a small space between each area of colour. Leaving this space gives a crisp outline between the colours.

TIP

Keep checking the front of the work to see that the loops are all the same height. If any loops are sitting higher, very gently and from the back of the work, push the fine crochet hook through the embroidery at the position of the higher loop, hook the loop and gently twist the crochet hook out of the fabric, thereby reducing the length of the loop until it is flush with all of the others. Not having the fabric sufficiently tight in the hoop can cause loops to be uneven in length.

Finishing

Check the completed piece to see that all the loops on the front are even. Use the crochet hook to carefully pull longer loops through to the back if necessary.

Remove the fabric from the hoop and pull it into shape.

Trim the ends of the threads on the back.

On the back, smear You Can Wash It craft glue over the outside two rows of the embroidery and onto the surrounding fabric, ensuring that the glue penetrates the fibres, and leave to dry.

Assembly

Carefully cut the completed embroidery away from the backing fabric. Take special care not to cut any of the loops on the outside edge. If loops are cut accidentally they can be glued and pushed into place by a very tiny amount of glue applied with a pin or needle tip.

Stitch or glue the tortoises in place on the baby capsule cover, and leave to dry.

Traditional punchneedle embroidery launders very well, so is perfect to decorate an item such as a small baby blanket.

FIVE FABULOUS DAISIES

The versatility of punchneedle embroidery is showcased in the beauty of this glorious bouquet of silk ribbon daisies and flowers. The lustrous yellow button flowers in Rajmahal art silks add a bright accent to this superb arrangement.

Tracing guide

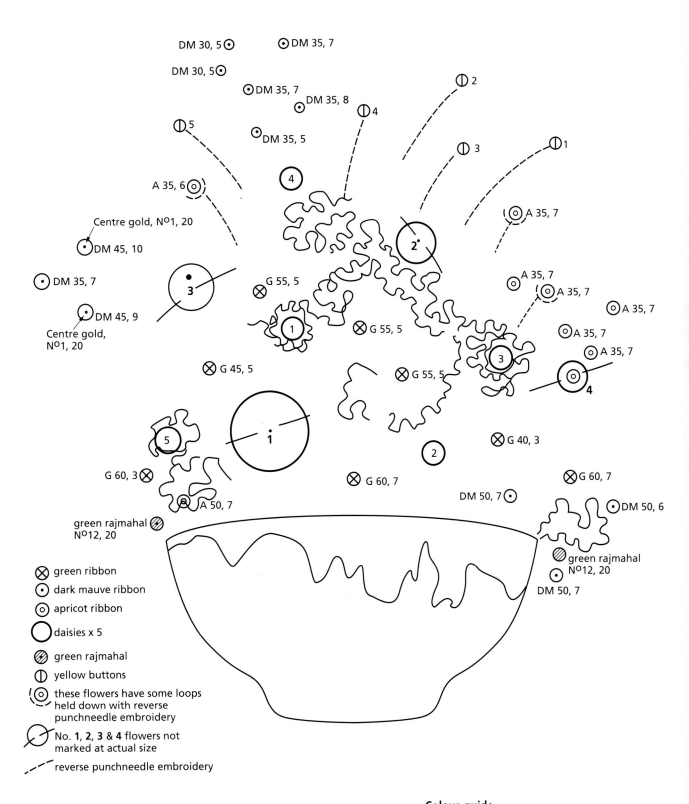

DM 30, 5 ⊙   ⊙ DM 35, 7

DM 30, 5 ⊙

⊙ DM 35, 7

⊙ DM 35, 8

DM 35, 5

Ⓘ 2

Ⓘ 4

Ⓘ 5

Ⓘ 3

Ⓘ 1

A 35, 6 ⊚

④

②

⊙ A 35, 7

Centre gold, Nº1, 20

⊙ DM 45, 10

③

G 55, 5

A 35, 7

A 35, 7

⊙ DM 35, 7

G 55, 5

A 35, 7

A 35, 7

DM 45, 9

①

A 35, 7

Centre gold,
Nº1, 20

③

G 45, 5

G 55, 5

④

i

⑤

G 40, 3

②

G 60, 3

G 60, 7

G 60, 7

A 50, 7

DM 50, 7 ⊙

DM 50, 6

green rajmahal
Nº12, 20

green rajmahal
Nº12, 20

DM 50, 7

⊗ green ribbon

⊙ dark mauve ribbon

⊚ apricot ribbon

◯ daisies x 5

⊘ green rajmahal

Ⓘ yellow buttons

⊚ these flowers have some loops
held down with reverse
punchneedle embroidery

No. **1**, **2**, **3** & **4** flowers not
marked at actual size

- - - reverse punchneedle embroidery

Colour guide

Materials

Dancing Ribbon needle

medium punchneedle

*7 mm (just over ¼ in) Kakoonda hand-dyed silk
    ribbon:*

    pale variegated mauve 3C

    darker mauve 5A

    variegated apricot 101

    darker apricot 310

    white

    green 306

Rajmahal art silks:

    persimmon 144

    green earth 421

    baby camel 45

*35 cm (14 in) square fabric of tightly woven fabric
    suitable to allow the use of the Dancing
    Ribbon needle*

small metal ruler

25 cm (10 in) lip-lock hoop

22.5 cm (9 in) square of fabric

*15 cm (6 in) hoop (used for working three daisies
    and the small flower at the base of the bowl)*

designer fabric to arrange under the bowl

*terracotta bowl 10 x 5.5 cm (4 x 2 ¼ in), flat-
    backed*

water-erasable pen

crochet hook

You Can Wash it craft glue

doughnut of fabric (see Chapter 3 Techniques)

*iron-on woven interfacing, optional (see Chapter 2
    Requirements)*

Preparation

Iron the ribbons and fabric.

If using iron-on interfacing, iron it onto the back of the chosen fabric.

Trace the design onto the back of the fabric.

A few stems, indicated on the pattern by lines of dashes, are worked in reverse punchneedle embroidery. Mark these onto the front of the fabric with the water-erasable pen.

Assemble the fabric in the hoop and tighten very firmly.

Iron interfacing onto the second piece of fabric if necessary. This is the piece the three daisies and the small flower at the base of the bowl are embroidered on.

Embroidery

Six strands of Rajmahal art silk are used throughout the design.

TIP

It is not necessary to cut the ribbon at the end of each round. Simply pull the needle along the ribbon, measure the new needle length and then pull the ribbon from the handle to tighten the ribbon again before beginning the next round.

No 1 Flower

The centre

1st round Set the medium punchneedle at No 1 and with the baby camel thread embroider 20 stitches in a circle (see Stitch Glossary, Figure 5).

Draw a line with the water-erasable pen to show where the next rounds start and end.

2nd round Set the punchneedle at No 3 and work all the way around the 1st row. It is not necessary to count the number of stitches worked around the centre circle.

3rd round Set the punchneedle at No 5 and work all the way around.

4th round Set the punchneedle at No 7 and work all the way around.

TIP

The centre of the flower needs to be quite large, as when the ribbon loops are embroidered they tend to encroach on the centre which cannot be seen if it's too small. For visual effect it is preferable that at least some of the centre can be seen. Measure the circle across the diameter on the back of the fabric, making sure it is at least 15 mm. Another row or two of stitching can be embroidered to make up the required size.

Ribbon loops Work with the Dancing Ribbon Needle, using the pale mauve variegated ribbon. (Refer to box, The Dancing Ribbon Needle, with the project Beautiful Brooches.)

Mark the position for the 20 petals onto the fabric (see diagram 1).

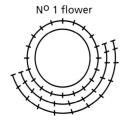

NO 1 flower

Marking placement for ribbon loops.

Diagram 1

1st round With needle tip measuring 40mm (1 ⅝ in) work 20 stitches all the way around the centre.

2nd round Mark positions for 12 petals 2 mm (¹⁄₁₆ in) away from the previous row of ribbon stitches. Measure the needle tip at 50 mm (2 in) and work the 12 stitches.

3rd round Mark 12 petals, 2 mm (¹⁄₁₆ in) away from the previous round, and with the needle tip measured at 60 mm (2 ⅜ in) work the 12 stitches.

No 2 Flower

Centre Use the medium punchneedle and baby camel thread.

1st round Set the punchneedle at No 1 and work 16 stitches in a circle.

Note 2nd, 3rd, and 4th rounds are worked only three-quarters of the way around the centre circle to the line shown on the diagram (see diagram 2).

2nd round Worked with the needle set at No 3.

3rd round Worked with the needle set at No 5.

4th round Worked with the needle set at No 7.

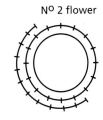

NO 2 flower

Marking placement for ribbon loops.

Diagram 2

Ribbon loops Work with the Dancing Ribbon Needle, using the pale mauve variegated ribbon.

1st round Mark the position of 16 petals 2 mm (¹⁄₁₆ in) away from the centre. Measure the needle tip at 40 mm (1 ⅝ in) to work the loops.

2nd round With the needle set at 50 mm (2 in), mark the positions for 12 petals, to the line marked on the pattern, 2mm (¹⁄₁₆ in) from the previous row.

No 3 Flower

Centre Embroider the centre the same as No 2 flower.

Ribbon loops Work as No 2 flower, with pale apricot ribbon.

No 4 Flower

Centre Work the centre the same as for No 2 flower.

Ribbon loops

1st round Mark the position of 16 petals. Measure the needle tip at 40mm (1 ⅝ in) and work 10 loops to the line shown on the pattern. Change the needle tip to 30 mm (1 ⅛ in) to work the remaining 6 loops of this round.

2nd round With the needle set at 50 mm (2 in), mark the position to the marked line on the pattern for 10 petals 2 mm (¹⁄₁₆ in) from the previous row.

Dark mauve flowers

These 12 flowers are marked DM on the pattern, where it also shows the length to measure the needle and the number of loops to make for each individual flower.

The length and number of stitches are indicated on the pattern as, for example, DM, 30, 7. This means that for flower DM the needle tip is measured at 30 mm (1 ⅛ in), with 7 stitches being made.

Apricot flowers

Embroider these eight flowers (marked A) in the same way as the dark mauve flowers.

Three of the apricot flowers are treated a little differently, with reverse punchneedle embroidery stitched over their base. These are marked on the pattern with a curved line of dashes.

With the medium punchneedle set at No 3 and using six strands of Rajmahal green 421, work reverse punchneedle embroidery (see Stitch Glossary, Figure 3) over the centre 3 long loops of these flowers, at least 2 mm (¹⁄₁₆ in) from the base of each loop toward the centre. See the pattern for the position of the loops to be worked over. If the reverse punchneedle stitching is not worked far enough up from the base of the loops, the loops will not be held down enough to give a good effect. When working these reverse punchneedle embroidery stitches, very gently twist the needle-tip through the already worked area and punch between each ribbon loop.

Work a further row of reverse punchneedle embroidery directly under the row just worked.

Work back to the centre underneath the second row. Change the needle tip to No1 and from that centre position, with reverse punchneedle embroidery, stitch in the stem.

Yellow button flowers

Use the bright yellow thread to embroider these five flowers.

Flower 1 Set the punchneedle at No 5. Work 20 stitches in a circle (see Stitch Glossary, Figure 5). The following four rows are worked around the centre circle, changing the needle for each row, from No 4 down to No 1.

Flower 2 Set the punchneedle at No 4. Work 20 stitches in a circle. The following three rows are worked around the centre circle, changing the needle for each row, from No 3 down to No 1.

Flower 3 Set the punchneedle at No 3. Work 20 stitches in a circle. The following two rows are worked around the centre circle, changing the needle for each row, from No 2 down to No 1.

Flowers 4 and 5 Set the punchneedle at No 2. Work 20 stitches in a circle. The following row is worked around the centre circle at No 1.

Silk ribbon greenery

Follow the placement for the seven bunches of green ribbon greenery (marked G in the pattern). Instructions for each bunch are on the pattern.

When the design is completed it is acceptable to add some extra fill-in areas of green where necessary to give an overall appealing look.

Background greenery

Set the punchneedle at No 3 to work with six strands of green Rajmahal thread. It is worked in a meandering fashion (see Stitch Glossary, Figure 9) to fill in the background spaces. If the area looks too sparse at completion, embroider bigger areas than shown on the pattern.

Daisies

Three daisies, Nos 1, 2, and 3 are embroidered onto a separate piece of fabric. Leave a space to embroider the flower at the foot of the bowl. (Daisies Nos 4 and 5 are embroidered onto the main piece of fabric.)

TIP

If the daisies were embroidered into the body of the design, they would look as though they are all facing directly upwards and not have any 'movement' to them within the completed piece of work. By embroidering them on a separate piece of fabric, cutting them out and placing them individually into the body of the work, they are more effective.

Daisies Nos 1, 2 and 3

Assemble the 22.5 cm (9 in) square of fabric tightly in the hoop to embroider these three daisies.

Centres Set the medium punchneedle at No 5. Work 20 stitches in a circle with the bright yellow thread. The three following rows to complete the centre are worked at No 4, 3, and 2.

Ribbon loops Work in the white ribbon with the Dancing Ribbon needle measured at 65 mm (2 ⅝ in) and work around the centre with 14 stitches, leaving a small space between the ribbon row and the centre.

Flower at foot of bowl

Work the flower with pale mauve variegated ribbon with 6 stitches in a circle with the needle tip at 40 mm (1 ⅝ in).

To finish the work on the separate piece of fabric

Trim the ends of the thread and ribbon. On the back, glue over the embroidered stitches and 6 mm (¼ in) around the stitches. It is important that the glue penetrates the fibres of the fabric so that fraying doesn't occur when the flowers are cut out. However, take care that the glue doesn't seep right through the fabric and onto the silk ribbon. Leave to dry before removing the work from the hoop.

With care, and holding the silk ribbon loops out of the way, cut the four flowers away from the fabric close to the embroidery.

Daisies 4 and 5

These are embroidered the same as daisies 1, 2, 3 on their marked positions on the main fabric piece.

Completing the five daisies

Hold onto each loop and with sharp scissors cut the top of the loop into a point and at the same time cut the loop apart so two separate petals are formed. See diagram 3. For the very top daisy, No 4, the loops are cut a little shorter than the others.

Cutting the top of the loops to form the daisy petals.

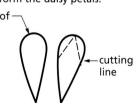

Diagram 3

When positioning daisies Nos 1, 2 and 3, take due care to prevent getting glue onto any ribbon loops. With a small amount of glue on the back of the daisies, position them in place as shown on the pattern. These daisies are placed onto the loops of meandering green background, which helps to raise them. Place the daisies sideways in various directions. The daisies need to be propped into position until they dry.

Finishing

Remove the work from the hoop and carefully press around the outside of the embroidery.

Stitch the separate designer fabric into place under the bowl.

The shadow painted on the bowl is optional. It has, though, been painted with Jo Sonja paints with equal parts of grey and amethyst with the slightest touch of blue added.

Wrap two wraps of the bright yellow thread around the bottom rim of the bowl and secure them on the back with a small piece of tape or a smear of glue.

Glue the bowl into place, pushing it up under the ribbon loops so that they can flow over the top.

Stitch or glue the small mauve flower to the left of the bowl.

This lovely ribbon embroidery will need to be framed in a box frame to protect it and to prevent the ribbon loops from becoming squashed.

GRACEFUL LAVENDER

This appealing lavender design has been embroidered with pretty multi-toned cotton thread. Set in a round mount with a background of many pastel shades, this piece will hang gracefully on any wall.

Requirements

small and medium punchneedles

25 cm (10 in) lip-lock embroidery hoop

40 cm (15 in) square of good-quality woven fabric

water-erasable pen

To colour the background (optional), sharpened
*   Derwent watercolour pencils:*
*   juniper green 42*
*   magenta 22*
*   cedar green 50*
*   olive green 51*
*   imperial purple 23*
*   blue violet lake 27*
*   may green 48*
*   deep cadmium 6*
*   sap green 49*
*   blue 30*
OR rainbow-coloured iron-on transfer paper (see
*   Techniques)*
wide paintbrush
clean water

Threads

Needle Necessities overdyed 6-stranded
*   embroidery threads*
*   Coventry gardens 178*
*   Grecian olive 142*

	Madeira	DMC
pale green	*1513*	*522*
dark green	*1514*	*520*
mid green	*1601*	*3362*
green	*1605*	*3013*

TIP

Cut a 15 cm (6 in) circle from clear acetate and place this over the bordering circle of the design when the fabric has been stretched tight in the hoop. Pull the fabric to shape, using the acetate as a template to ensure that the embroidery is being done on a true circle shape.

Preparation

Please note that in this design there are a number of stems where the embroidery is worked from the front of the piece. These stems are marked on the pattern sheet as lines of dashes. These are worked in reverse punchneedle embroidery (see Stitch Glossary, Figure 3), whereby the beautiful little running stitch that is normally worked on the back of the fabric is embroidered on the front. The loops are then formed on the back of the fabric. Reverse punchneedle embroidery emulates the traditional embroidery stitch known as stem stitch.

There are two methods for colouring the fabric, either with rainbow transfer paper or water colour pencils. Iron a 25 cm (10 in) circle of the coloured transfer paper (see Chapter 3 Techniques) onto the centre of the front of the fabric, or colour the background by another preferred method.

The outside edge is embroidered on the front with overstitching reverse punchneedle embroidery (see Special Effects, sample e, p53).

Using watercolour pencils

Draw a 25 cm (10 in) circle onto the centre of the chosen fabric as shown on the design sheet. Assemble the fabric into the hoop, as it is easier to colour-in on fabric when it is held tight in the hoop. The fabric is coloured on the side that will be the completed front. Holding the pencil at an angle so that only the side of the coloured tip is on the fabric, colour the fabric in a manner similar to that shown in the accompanying photograph, to the depth of colour that suits. Colour the fabric darker in the bottom third, a little lighter in the mid third and much lighter in the top third. Moisten the paintbrush with clean water, dry it off on a clean cloth or tissue and gently brush over the pencil colours.

Tracing guide

Enlarge at 110%

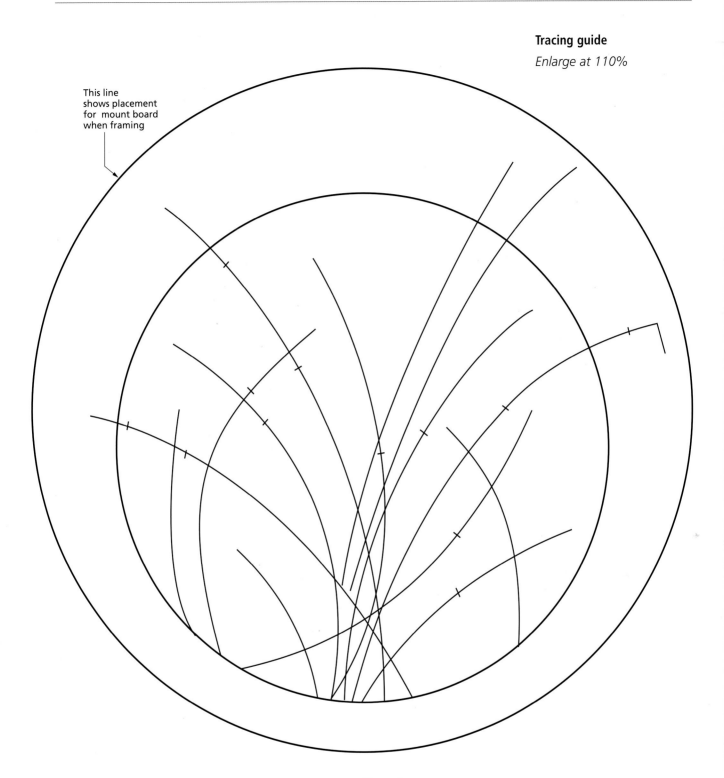

This line
shows placement
for mount board
when framing

The moisture will cause the colours to merge into each other. With care, add depth to the colour where needed by adding more colour and brushing again. Remove the fabric from the hoop when dry.

Tracing

Trace the design onto the back of the fabric using your preferred method of transferring a design.

Assemble the fabric very tightly in the hoop with the traced design facing down. Turn the hoop over and with a lead pencil or water-

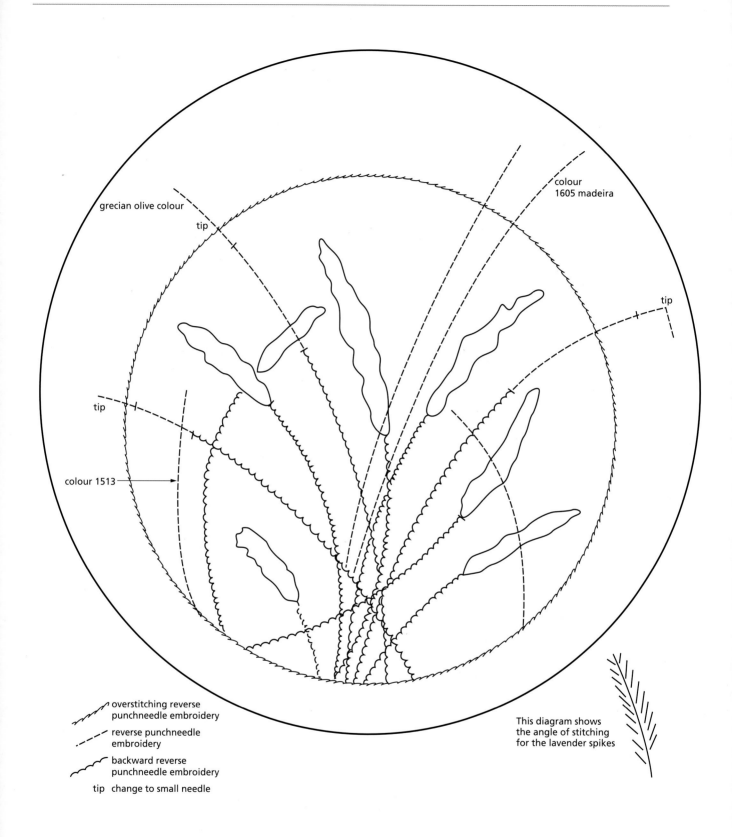

grecian olive colour

tip

colour
1605 madeira

tip

tip

colour 1513

overstitching reverse
punchneedle embroidery

reverse punchneedle
embroidery

backward reverse
punchneedle embroidery

tip change to small needle

This diagram shows
the angle of stitching
for the lavender spikes

Stitch and colour guide

erasable pen lightly mark all the stems and outside circle edge onto the front of the fabric. Do this by holding the design up to a well-lit window or over a light box so that you can see the markings easily.

Embroidery

Lavender spikes

Work with three strands of the variegated Needle Necessities thread 178 through the small needle set at No 1. See the small diagram at the right of the Colour and Stitch Guide.

Punch the needle into the fabric at the end of the lavender spike tip. Work two small stitches backward and then work forward directly over the stitches just made.

Work a stitch out to the left and then work another stitch over the top of that stitch immediately back to the centre.

Repeat out to the right.

Work one stitch forward.

Repeat one stitch to the left and back to the centre and then out to the right and back to the centre.

Work two stitches forward and then two stitches out to the left. Return to the centre by working over the previously punched stitches.

Repeat two stitches out to the right.

Continue in this manner for three pairs of outward stitching.

Now work two stitches forward and then three stitches out to the left. Return to the centre by working over the previously punched stitches. Repeat out to the right.

Work 3 or 4 pairs like this and then increase the number of stitches outward to four for 2, 3 or 4 pairs, depending on the length of the spike. Decrease the number of stitches outward toward the bottom of the spike until it is completed.

Note These instructions give the basic way of embroidering a lavender spike, particularly the biggest spike in this design. It may be that the smaller spikes will only require two or three stitches outward on either side. Use the pattern as a guide for the size of the completed lavender spikes.

The outside edges of the spikes need to be random, not smooth, for a natural effect.

Lavender stems

Use three strands each of Madeira 1513 and 1601 (or DMC 522 and 3362) together through the medium needle set at No 1. On the front, work the stems in backward reverse punchneedle embroidery (see Special Effects, Sample h, p54). Remember to pull the starting and finishing threads through to the back.

Thick grasses

Work these in reverse punchneedle embroidery with six strands of Needle Necessities Grecian Olive 142 in the medium needle at No 1, starting where indicated on the pattern and working to the base of the stem. With backward reverse punchneedle embroidery embroider directly alongside, on the left, of the row previously embroidered. Work to the finish line as indicated on the pattern. Punch the last stitch into a stitch of the previous row.

Change to the small needle and three strands of Madeira 1513 (DMC 522). Punch in the tips of the stems with fine reverse punchneedle embroidery, matching the last stitch with the first of the previous stitching.

Fine grasses

Change to the small needle and three strands of Madeira 1605 (DMC 3013) to embroider these two stems with fine reverse punchneedle embroidery.

Remaining stems

Change to the small needle and three strands of Madeira 1513 (DMC 522) and embroider the remaining stems with fine reverse punchneedle embroidery.

Outside circle

This is embroidered in overstitching reverse punchneedle embroidery (see Special Effects, sample e, p53).

Avoid embroidering over the grasses by stopping and starting before and after you get to each grass stem. Take the start and finish threads through to the back.

Finishing

Mark the background lavenders shown in the Pencil Colour Guide and with the colour pencils lightly colour the spikes on the front of the fabric.

Draw the background grasses with green.

Trim threads on the back.

Remove the embroidery from the hoop and stretch the fabric in all directions to straighten out the grain.

Mount this in a delicate gold frame with an offset round matt board.

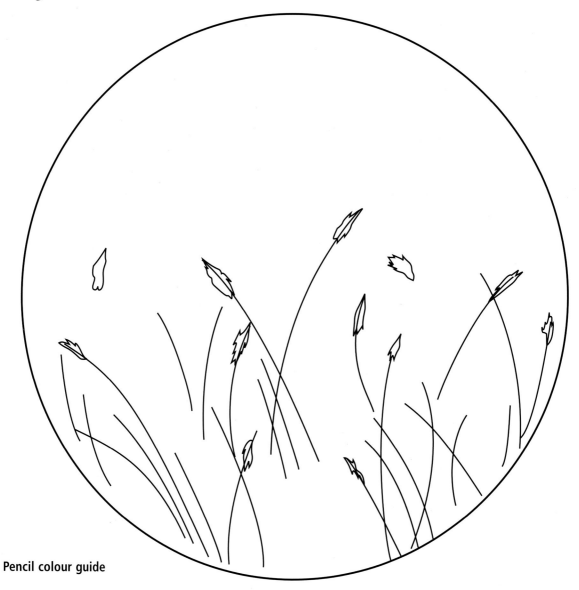

Pencil colour guide

SHAGGY BEAR WITH HIS BLUE BOW

This adorable, shaggy golden bear with his blue bow is embroidered using the punchneedle embroidery technique in which each loop formed is cut to give him his shaggy look. He will become a favourite for almost anyone who sees him and looks equally cute and cuddly on a child's sweater or in a frame.

Materials

large punchneedle

25 cm (10 in) lip-lock hoop

40 cm (15 in) square of fabric

sharp embroidery scissors

iron-on transfer pen

acrylic yarn holder

acrylic yarn, Cameo brand, as listed below

8 mm (⁵⁄₁₆ in) amber glass eyes

small glass bear nose

coloured bow

Cameo yarns

   harvest gold 48

   antique gold 47

   light brown 60

This shaggy bear is worked with two thicknesses of acrylic yarn through the large punchneedle. If only one spool of a colour is available, wind a large amount of the yarn from the spool around a strong piece of cardboard, and cut, then thread

Tracing guide

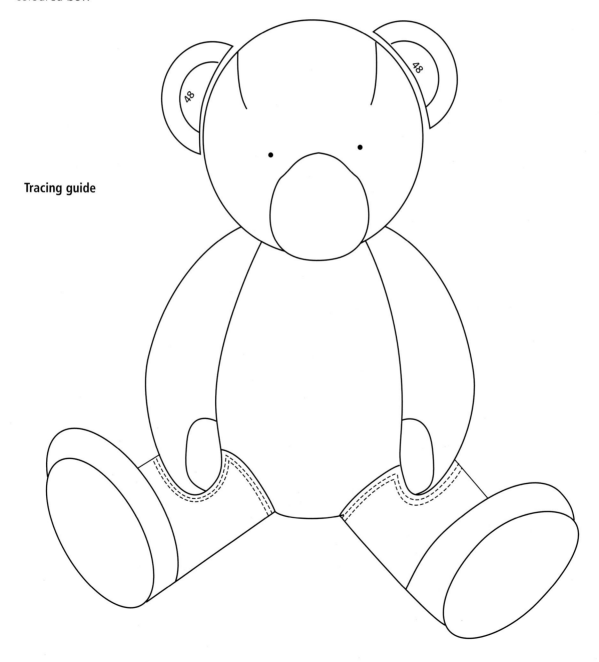

the ends of both lengths of yarn through the large needle tip. Ideally, working with two spools on a yarn holder is easier, as the yarn then flows smoothly and evenly.

Preparation

Trace the design onto the back of the fabric (see Chapter 3 Techniques).

Unlike most other punchneedle embroidery, for this design the traced pattern is put into the hoop facing down. You will be embroidering from inside the hoop, which is not the usual way. The loops made will thus be on top of the hoop, making them easier to cut.

Assemble the fabric into the hoop. Ensure that the fabric is extremely taut and the hoop nut is done up very tightly. If the fabric is not sufficiently tight, the loops will be uneven in length.

Embroidery

Read about the Shaggy Look in Chapter 5 Another Dimension.

To give the best effect for the shaggy look, the stitches on the back are worked at least a large needle-width in length and each row a little away from the previous. It is not necessary for the punched loops to be as close together as usual because when they are cut they need room to 'fluff' out.

Work only one row of stitches before turning the work over and cutting each loop. Pull each loop up to its full height with the scissors and then cut it open. This is important to ensure that the 'fluff' is mostly at the same level and not too shaggy and uneven. Ensure that each loop is cut. There is a marked colour difference where some loops are left uncut. A good light helps to pick up loops which have missed the cutting process.

The main parts of the bear are worked with colour 47, antique gold.

Muzzle

The bear's muzzle is worked in the colour 47, antique gold, with the outside casing removed from the punchneedle, leaving the full length of the needle tip exposed (see Long Loops in Chapter 3 Techniques).

Here the loops are made with the full length of the exposed needle tip. Punch each loop the full depth of the exposed needle, that is, all the way to the blue hilt of the needle. Cut each row after it is worked. When all the loops have been cut, the area of the muzzle (nose and mouth) needs to be trimmed. Use the sharp, pointed scissors at an angle of nearly 45 degrees from the top of the nose towards the cheeks.

Shape the area with gentle trimming. Learning to roll the scissors as you trim gives a lovely rounded effect. If by accident too much cutting occurs, simply punch in further loops and re-trim.

The glass nose is glued onto the finished muzzle.

Eye area

Embroider 10 stitches in a circle (see Stitch Glossary, Figure 5) in colour 47, antique gold, with the needle tip set at No 5. These loops are not cut. The glass amber eyes are glued on top of the loops.

Head

The line on either side of the forehead is worked in colour 48, harvest gold, with the punchneedle set at No 10. Stitch two rows and cut the loops.

Indicated on the pattern is a space between the ears and the head. Leave this space un-worked.

The remaining parts of the head are worked with the punchneedle set at No 12 and in colour 47, antique gold.

Ears

Set the punchneedle at No 12 and embroider the outside areas with colour 47, antique gold.

The inner sections are worked in colour 48, harvest gold, with the punchneedle set at No10.

Arms

Set the punchneedle at No 11 and with colour 47, antique gold embroider two rows at the outer edge. Fill in the remaining area at No 12.

Paw pads These are embroidered in colour 60, light brown, with the needle tip set at No 10. The stitching for the paws is worked slightly closer than for the rest of the body, which will give a more velvety look as opposed to the shaggy look when trimmed. Trim around the pads to define the shape.

Body

Work all around the body area with two rows at No 8 with colour 48, harvest gold, then fill the body area with 47, antique gold, first working two rows at No 9, then two rows at No 10, two rows at No 11, and filling in the remaining area at No 12.

Cut the loops of each row as it is completed.

Legs

Work with colour No 48, harvest gold, and set the punchneedle at No 8 to work two rows at the top of the leg and around the paws, indicated on the pattern by the dotted lines. *Complete the feet* before filling the remaining area of each leg with No 47, antique gold, with the punchneedle set at No 8.

Feet

Paw pads Start at the outside edge and work two rows in 60, light brown, with the needle tip set at No 5.

For the next three rows set the needle tip at No 6. Fill in the remaining area with the needle tip set at No 7. The bottom edges of the paws are treated in the same manner as the front paws above.

Top of foot Starting next to the paw, using 47, antique gold, set the needle tip at No 8 and work two rows. Change to No 9 and work two rows; finally, change to No 10 and work two rows.

Now go back and fill in the remaining leg area at No 8.

Finishing

Before removing the bear from the hoop, pin it up on a board to view it. This gives you the opportunity to check whether the finished piece looks 'good' or needs re-arranging. This is particularly so for the muzzle area.

Trim and tidy the outer edges if necessary.

Check that all the loops have been cut.

Glue the amber glass eyes and nose in place.

Stitch a bow into place.

Glue the outside edges of stitching on the back. Leave to dry.

Carefully cut the bear away from the fabric which it was worked on.

This delightful bear can be framed or attached to a child's sweater.

BEAR IN A GARDEN

This lovable bear is embroidered using a fascinating technique in which long punched loops are cut and sculpted. The background is easily coloured with iron-on transfer paper and the garden is made from tumbled rock fragments and punch-embroidered flowers.

Requirements

large punchneedle

medium punchneedle for the flowers

25 cm (10 in) lip-lock hoop

15 cm (6 in) lip-lock hoop

35 cm (14 in) square of fabric coloured with iron-on transfer paper (optional); see Techniques

25 cm (9 in) square of fabric onto which the flowers are embroidered

small, sharp, pointed embroidery scissors

You Can Wash It craft glue

iron-on transfer pen

tapestry needle

2 Mill Hill petite glass beads, gold 40557

small red bow (optional)

spotted ribbon for braces (optional)

Tracing guide

Acrylic yarn

	Cameo	Pretty Punch
beige	*54*	*43*
taupe	*59*	*29*
royal blue	*12*	*49*
black	*1*	*58*

DMC threads for flowers

brown 938

yellow 90

yellow 3078

pink 1203

TIP

Be aware that acrylic yarn colours change to a deeper shade when loops are cut.

Preparation

TIP

Sculpting (see Chapter 5 Another Dimension) is a technique whereby punched loops are cut and shaped which results in a plush, velvet-like appearance. Practice with this technique to achieve stunning results. The good thing is that it is a very forgiving technique, for if the results are not pleasing it is easy to remove what has been done and to re-stitch an area.

If a mistake is made and too many loops have been cut, simply embroider some more loops and cut the loops again.

Colour the front of the fabric with randomly-torn pieces of iron-on transfer paper as described in Chapter 3 Techniques, and using the photograph as a guide.

Trace the pattern onto the back of the large fabric square.

TIP

Unlike most other punchneedle embroidery designs, this traced pattern is put into the hoop facing down. You will be embroidering from inside the hoop, which is not the usual way. The loops made will thereby be on top of the hoop which makes them easier to cut and sculpt.

Assemble the fabric into the hoop, ensuring that the fabric is extremely taut and the hoop nut is done up very tightly.

Embroidery

This design is embroidered with two thicknesses of acrylic yarn through a large punchneedle. If only one spool of a colour is available, wind a large amount of the yarn from the spool around a strong piece of cardboard, and cut, then thread the ends of both thicknesses of yarn through the large needle tip. Ideally, working with two spools on a yarn holder is easier, as the yarn then flows smoothly and evenly.

Set the punchneedle at No 12. The whole of the bear (except for the nose area and the eyes) is worked at No 12.

Leave a space between each area, as indicated on the pattern. This space allows the scissors to be moved between each area for sculpting and trimming.

The paws and inside area of the ears are worked in Cameo taupe 59 (or Pretty Punch 29). The remainder of the bear is embroidered with Cameo beige 54 (or Pretty Punch 43).

Eyes

The eyes are worked first, using two strands of black yarn through the large needle. Set the punchneedle at No 10 and punch 15 stitches in a circle (see Stitch Glossary, Figure 5). These loops are not cut.

TIP

The next step involves wrapping yarn around the formed loops of the eye. Why? Completed long loops take up more area on the front than the area stitched on the back (see Stitch Glossary, Figure 2, sample e).

Wrapping thread around the loops contains them within a smaller space which prevent them getting tangled with the cut areas. Wrapped loops like this also give eyes or a nose better definition.

Thread the sewing needle with black yarn, double the yarn, and tie a knot at the end. Insert the needle from the outside row of the eye at the back of the fabric and push the needle to the front. From the base of the black loops, wrap the yarn four times around the loops in an upward spiral, pulling the yarn tight, which will close all the loops together. Take the needle through to the back at the base of the loops and fasten off the thread (see photograph a, b, c.)

The small gold beads are stitched into the eyes at about the 11 o'clock position once the face is completed.

Nose

The nose is worked in the same manner as the eyes but using a much longer needle tip. Remove the casing and spring from the large needle tip and handle and store away safely. (see Long Loops in Chapter 3 Techniques). Punch the very long needle tip all the way to the hilt of the needle and punch 30 stitches in a circle. These loops are not cut. Thread the sewing needle with black yarn, double the yarn, and tie a knot at the end. Insert the needle from the outside of the nose at the back of the fabric and push the needle through to the front. From the base, wrap the yarn six times around the loops in an upward spiral, pulling the yarn tight, which will close all the loops together. Insert the needle through to the back at the base of the loops and fasten off the thread. (See photograph a, b, c.)

Ears and face

These are the next parts to be embroidered.

Muzzle

The area surrounding the black nose is also worked with the casing removed from the handle of the needle with Cameo beige 54 (or Pretty Punch 43). Cut each row as it is worked (see photograph d.) When all of the loops have been cut, the area of the muzzle needs to be trimmed. Use the sharp, pointed scissors at an angle from the top of the nose towards the cheeks.

Shape the area with gentle trimming, rolling the scissors while trimming to give a lovely rounded effect (see photograph e.) If by accident too much cutting occurs, simply punch in further loops and re-trim.

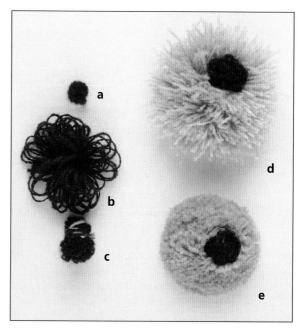

Left side shows how to wrap long loops to form a nose or eyes, right side shows how to shape a bear muzzle.

a   *Punched area on the back.*

b   *Long loops formed on the front.*

c   *Long loops wrapped. The white thread can be seen encircling the loops, pulling them tightly together.*

d   *Cut loops.*

e   *Sculpted and shaped muzzle.*

TIP

Getting a 'good' look to a bear's muzzle area is one of the most difficult things to achieve with the sculpting technique of punchneedle embroidery. Take time to practise and be warned that it seems as though the trimming will go on forever—-there always seems to be 'just a bit more' that needs to be tidied and trimmed. A light mist of hairspray will hold the trimmed fur in place.

Mouth

Take two strands of yarn about 15 cm (6 in) in length. Tie a knot at one end and pull the end tag very tightly. Check that it is very secure. Cut the end tag very close to the knot.

Make another knot 12 mm (a little less than ½ in) from the first knot. Pull tightly to secure the knot and cut off the long tag, leaving you with a small piece of black thread tied with a knot at both ends. Place this into position for the mouth. First dab a little glue onto the centre of the thread for the mouth and set this in place on the cut fur. Leave to dry.

When quite dry, put a small dab of glue on one end under the knot. Press the knot in place a little higher than the level at which the mouth has been attached at the centre, making a curve to the thread. Leave to dry. Repeat for the other side, matching the curve. Forming the curve will give the bear a lovely smile.

Body

This is worked with the punchneedle set at No 12, using Cameo beige 54 (or Pretty Punch 43).

The pattern shows a space left between each body part. These spaces are left unworked, which allows the scissors to more easily get in and around the body parts for cutting and sculpting.

Punch each section, cutting the loops of each row open as it is completed.

Trim and shape each of the body areas as they are worked. Where edges need to be rounded, sculpt to shape by holding the scissors at a gentle angle and carefully trimming the edges.

Glide the scissors into the spaces not worked. This makes it easier to trim and sculpt.

Clip into the indents of the forehead.

Work the pants in Cameo royal blue 12 (or Pretty Punch royal blue 49) and sculpt as you go.

The cutting causes lots of fluff. If possible, cut onto a sheet of plastic or fabric so that all the mess can be gathered up. Clap your hand onto the hoop periodically as though playing the tambourine to remove excess fluff.

Leave the fabric tight in the hoop as you trim and sculpt.

Flowers and grass

These are embroidered on the smaller piece of fabric with the medium needle and six strands of DMC embroidery cotton. Assemble the fabric into the smaller hoop. See Stitch Glossary, Figure 5, for working flowers.

Yellow flowers The centre is made with brown 938 with the needle tip set at No 3 and 20 stitches worked in a circle. Set the needle at No 2 to work all the way around the first row. Change to yellow 90 for the petals. Work all the way around the centre with the needle tip set at No 4, then change the needle tip to No 6 for the final row.

Pink flowers Make the centres with pale yellow 3078 with the needle tip set at No 1 and work 30 stitches in a circle. Change to pink 1203 and work all the way around the centre with the needle tip set at No 10.

Grass Remove the casing from the needle tip. Using green 3362, work 12 stitches in a circle.

Finishing

Trim any ends of thread on the back. Remove the fabric from the hoop to give the bear a final trim. Give the fabric a good shake to finally remove any remaining cut fibres.

Press around the embroidered bear, taking extra care that the iron does not slide over the cut 'fur'.

This delightful bear has been set in a garden.

Add further colour to the background fabric with randomly torn iron-on transfer paper, again taking care that the iron does not touch the fur. A hot iron can scorch the fur and leave marks, just like what happens when an iron is pressed onto velvet.

If you are giving the bear a bow and braces, stitch them into place now.

Glue the backs of the flowers and the grass. Leave to dry. Cut the shapes away from the backing fabric.

Cut open each loop of the grass.

Glue the flowers and grasses into place using the photograph as a guide to their placement.

Use various tumbled and polished rock chips to scatter around the bear. These may not be readily available in which case, collect some tiny pebbles, wash and dry them and scatter these. Glue each pebble into place.

Place fine wadding under the fabric before framing.

Frame and enjoy.

PATCH THE FLUFFY DOG

*The patch around his eye gives an endearing look to this adorable fluffy dog,
embroidered with 2-ply acrylic yarn which has the unique property that the
punched loops can be brushed to give a soft fluffy appearance.*

Materials

medium punchneedle

25 cm (10 in) lip-lock embroidery hoop

40 cm (16 in) square of tightly woven fabric

fine, sharp scissors

iron-on transfer pen

wire fluffing brush

masking tape

10 mm (⅜ in) amber glass eyes (optional)

purchased black nose (optional)

You Can Wash It craft glue

Acrylic yarn

Cameo	Pretty Punch
white 2	*winter white 11*
black 1	*black 58*
dark brown 62	*dark brown 70*

Tracing and colour guide

indicates black

Preparation

Trace the design onto the fabric.

Unlike most other punchneedle embroidery, this design has the traced pattern put into the hoop facing down. The embroidery will be worked from inside the hoop, which is not the usual way. The loops made will thus be on top of the hoop, making them easier to brush. Assemble the fabric into the hoop. Ensure that the fabric is extremely taut and the hoop nut is done up very tightly.

Embroidery

TIPS

The formed loops are not cut before brushing and all fluffy areas are worked and brushed before any non-brushed areas are worked.

Only small sections are punched at a time—no more than 2.5–3.5 cm (1–1½ in) square. Punch and brush in a progressive manner.

Apart from two rows worked at No 1 around the eyes and nose, this design is worked with the needle tip set at No 2 and No 3 in different areas, as shown on the pattern.

When working at No 3, the punched stitches do not need to be extremely close together, as the brushing increases the overall volume and area covered.

TIP

When beginning and ending any area, backstitch (see Stitch Glossary, Figure 7) directly over the three previous stitches, or leave a long length of thread at the beginning and end. The reason for this is that when the brushing is done, the beginning and end yarn can very easily get caught in the bristles of the fluffing brush and some stitching may be pulled out. The long pieces of yarn are held in place with a finger while brushing to prevent their being snagged and pulled, and are trimmed afterwards. If during the brushing process, a

long end of thread does become unstitched, trim it before going on with any further brushing and then hold it in place on the back when brushing is resumed.

Embroidery

With the needle tip set at No 1, work two rows around the eyes and nose. Brush.

The remaining parts of the lower face are embroidered with the needle tip set at No 2.

The lines of dashes at the left side of the face and at the top of the fluffy head indicate where a single row of black is to be worked.

The line indicating the mouth area is worked with the needle tip set at No 1. Brush this row and then cut the brushed loops shorter, the reason for this being that only a hint of the mouth is necessary.

TIP

Turn the hoop over so that the flat surface of the fabric is uppermost for ease of brushing.

There is the possibility of damaging the fabric with the bristles of the wire brush. This can be overcome by the use of small pieces of masking tape shaped and pressed along the marked outline. A second row of tape may be required to increase the width of the protected area.

When brushing, hold the brush firmly by the wooden handle with the wire bristles angled toward you. Initially, hold the brush horizontal across the top of the loops and pull the metal teeth through the loops.

Press the brush firmly into the loops and drag the bristles through the loops.

Feel deep into the stitching with your fingers to check that all loops have been brushed out. Any lumps that can be felt indicate areas that have not been brushed sufficiently deeply.

The areas marked for the eyes and nose are not stitched if amber glass eyes or a purchased nose are to be glued into place.

Otherwise, embroider the eyes with dark brown starting on the outside edge with the needle tip set at No 1 and changing the length for each round until the area is filled in.

Patch looks even more adorable with a purchased nose but if one is not available his nose can be made in black with the 'shaping' technique (see Shaping in Chapter 5 Another Dimension). With the needle set at No 5 embroider a row of loops on the outside edge. Turn the hoop over and cut all of the loops open. Set the punchneedle at No 6 to embroider the next round. Cut the loops open. Fill in the nose area by increasing the needle tip for each round until the whole area is filled. Remember to cut the loops after each row. The nose may require some sculpting to give it a nice shape.

Finishing

When satisfied with the effect of your brushing, comb the fluff with the fluffing brush and use the needle tip to arrange the fluff to give a really 'doggie' appearance.

If purchased eyes and nose are used, glue them into the unworked spaces and leave to dry.

The fluffy look washes well, so it is possible to appliqué Patch to a garment to be worn. Alternatively, the embroidery can be framed.

JEWELLED WINGS

Jewelled Wings 1 shows a butterfly newly emerged from the cocoon as it wings its way in splendid jewelled colours into a world where we feast on the majesty of its vibrant new colours. The brilliance of this butterfly's appearance is achieved by embroidering with 2-ply acrylic yarn or three strands of embroidery cotton with the merest hint of gold.

Jewelled Wings 2 is embroidered from the same pattern but it has been given a vastly different finish by embroidering dots over the background colours. This version of the embroidery has been made into a miniature carpet.

Materials

medium punch-needle if using acrylic yarn

small punchneedle if using embroidery cotton

20 cm (8 in) lip-lock hoop

25 cm (10 in) square of fabric

sharp embroidery scissors

fine steel crochet hook

iron-on transfer pen

You Can Wash It craft glue

Acrylic yarns

This jewelled butterfly has been worked in Cameo yarns. While many of the colours in the Pretty Punch range have no direct match, I have chosen colours from this range which will work well together.

Cameo	Pretty Punch
green 27	*emerald green 66*
royal blue 12	*royal blue 49*
wine red 94	*cardinal 72*
magenta 15	*raspberry 6*
orange 73	*burnt orange 73*
black 1	*black 58*
antique gold 47	*antique gold 71*
grape 87	*grape 7*
peacock 75	*peacock 74*
teal 50	*jade 47*

Metallic gold Madeira 5014. The colour and brand are not important as this is only used for tiny highlights. Any gold metallic of a 6-strand equivalent can be used.

Threads

This design looks wonderful when embroidered with three strands of stranded embroidery cotton (floss) using a small punchneedle.

	DMC	Madeira
green	*910*	*1303*
blue	*796*	*913*
red	*498*	*704*
orange	*922*	*311*
gold	*781*	*2212*
purple	*550*	*2709*
peacock	*3812*	*2705*
teal	*943*	*2706*
black		
magenta	*915*	*705*
metallic gold	*5282*	*5014*

The direct DMC to Madeira colour conversions often are not a total match for a specific design. In this instance the colours have been coordinated and chosen as the best colours for the particular design. (Likewise, with the colour conversion from the acrylic range of colours to stranded cotton/floss.)

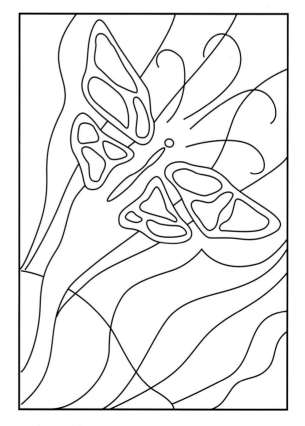

Tracing guide

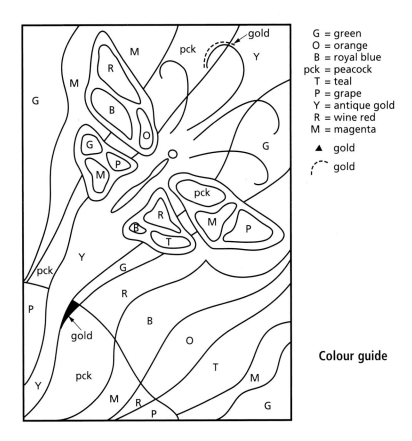

G = green
O = orange
B = royal blue
pck = peacock
T = teal
P = grape
Y = antique gold
R = wine red
M = magenta

▲ gold

⌒ gold

Colour guide

JEWELLED WINGS 1

Preparation

Trace the design onto the back of the fabric.

Place the fabric in the hoop with the traced design uppermost. Ensure that the fabric is extremely tight in the hoop.

Embroidery

The punchneedle is set at No 1 throughout for both the acrylic yarn and the stranded cotton.

Embroider the rectangular outline with two rows of unbroken loops in black.

Embroider the outer lines of the wings in two rows of black and outline the various colours on the wings of the butterfly with one row of black.

The antennae have only one row of black embroidery with the loops worked close together to give an unbroken line.

TIP

Work the loops very, very close together to achieve an unbroken line around the outside edge. This is a great tip for all punchneedle embroidery designs.

Wings

Embroider the different colours on the wings following the colour guide. Have a look at the photograph to check the placement of the colours.

Head

Work 10 stitches in a very tight circle in black (see Stitch Glossary, Figure 5).

Body

Fill in the body with black.

TIP

To get the very best effect for this design, it is important to leave a small space between each area of colour, which gives a crisp outline between the colours. If the space is not created, the loops of the adjoining colours become intermingled so that there is no definition of line and the shape is lost.

Embroider the background colours as indicated as shown on the colour guide.

Embroider the two tiny areas of gold metallic thread last of all.

Finishing

Check the completed piece to see that all of the loops on the front are even. Use the crochet hook to carefully pull longer loops through to the back if necessary.

Remove the fabric from the hoop. Pull the fabric into shape.

Trim the ends of the threads on the back.

This delightful piece looks marvellous when framed with a gold mount, which can be either a gold matt frame cut professionally or a padded fabric-covered mount.

TIP

Keep checking the front of the work to see that the loops are all the same height. If any loops are sitting higher, very gently, and from the back of the work, push the fine crochet hook through the embroidery at the place of the higher loop, hook the loop and gently twist the crochet hook out of the fabric, thereby reducing the length of the loop until it is flush with all of the others. Not having the fabric sufficiently tight in the hoop can cause uneven lengths of loops.

JEWELLED WINGS 2— a miniature carpet

Preparation

When transferring the design to the fabric, omit the rectangular border, instead putting only a dot in each corner. Trace the rest of the design onto the back of the fabric and then put the fabric in the hoop with the traced design uppermost. Ensure that the fabric is extremely tight in the hoop.

It is important with this piece of embroidery that the rectangular border is traced absolutely straight onto the fabric. The way to do this is to mark the straight grain of the fabric (see Chapter 3 Techniques) by scoring each side of the rectangle from corner to corner between the dots. The scored lines will then be perfectly straight on the grain of the fabric, ensuring that the completed miniature carpet looks entirely straight.

It is optional to mark over the scored lines lightly with a fine pen.

Embroidery

The embroidery is worked in basically the same way as Jewelled Wings 1 with the addition of dots embroidered near the edges of each colour change in the background (see Stitch Glossary, Figure 14), either as each section is completed or when all sections have been completed. Set the punchneedle at No 2. The colours for the dots are made with the colour taken from the adjacent section of colour. The dots are placed at random, with the stitches on the back being punched about 5–6 mm (¼ in) or so apart, which gives a nice spacing to the dots on the front of the embroidery.

The dots are only placed along the edges and a little way out from the edges. If the dots are not showing through the finished embroidery on the front, shorten the length of the stitches on the back. On the other hand, if the dots are sitting too high on the front of the fabric, you will need to lengthen the stitches on the back.

Keep checking the front as the embroidery progresses.

The gold is not used in this version.

TIP

When making dots, the needle tip is twisted gently to allow it to more easily penetrate the thickness of the previously embroidered loops.

Finishing

Check the completed piece to see that all of the loops on the front are even. Use the crochet hook to carefully pull any longer loops through to the back if necessary.

When the embroidery is complete, take the crochet hook and score the fabric 10 mm (slightly less than ⅜ in) from the two ends which will be fringed.

Remove the fabric from the hoop. Pull the fabric into shape.

Trim the ends of the threads on the back.

Very lightly, smear You Can Wash It craft glue over the entire back of the embroidery, taking care that the glue is kept away from the areas

where the thread will be drawn to make the fringed edge.

Leave to dry.

Carefully cut the completed embroidery away from the fabric, close to the two long sides and along the scored lines at the ends where the fringes will be made.

Fray the fibres of the fabric to make the fringe but leave 2 or 3 rows of fibres in place next to the embroidery.

This delightful miniature carpet can be framed or enjoyed as a colourful coaster for your morning cup of coffee.

IN A CORAL GARDEN

The underwater world of a coral reef comes to life with striking colours, many varied stitches and the optional addition of a little seahorse.

Embroidering this colourful underwater scene gives a greater understanding and appreciation of the many different effects that can be achieved when working with the punchneedle embroidery technique.

Requirements

small and medium punchneedles

20 cm (8 in) lip-lock embroidery hoop

two 30 cm (12 in) squares of fabric

iron-on transfer pen

seahorse charm (optional)

iron-on rainbow paper, pencils or fabric paints

You Can Wash It craft glue

2 mm piece of plastic to fit on the small
  punchneedle (see Pile Depth)

Threads

Some Madeira colours have no direct match with DMC colours. I have chosen colours from the DMC range which will work well together.

	Madeira	DMC
pale grey	1804	762
orange	207	946
chartreuse	1308	704
blue	906	793
purple	2710	333
sea green	1204	991
musty yellow	2513	972
burgundy	2608	3685
medium pink	411	3801
green	1612	732
dark purple	714	550
burnt orange	407	498

Madeira Glamour, a metallised effect yarn:

  turquoise 2466

  sea green 2465

  purple 2412

  This glitter thread can easily be substituted
  with any metallic thread in similar colours.

Needle Necessities overdyed cotton:

  floribunda 1791

  mayflowers 180

Note For this design any colour can be substituted and virtually any thread can be used so long as it flows freely through the eye of the punchneedle you have chosen.

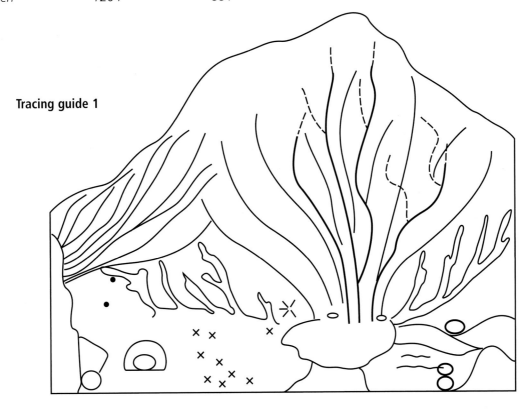

Tracing guide 1

Tracing guide 2

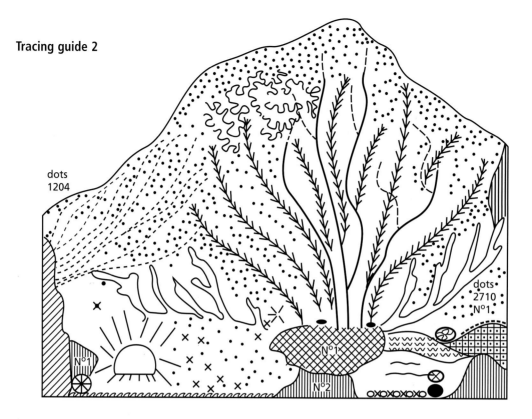

dots
1204

dots
2710
Nº1

Preparation

Iron the rainbow paper onto the front of the two pieces of fabric (see Chapter 3 Techniques); alternatively, softly colour the fabric with pencils or paint.

Transfer the main design from Tracing Guide 1 onto the back of one piece of fabric.

Use Tracing Guide 2 as further reference. There are areas of this design, indicated on the pattern, which need to be worked from the front. These lines need to be marked on the front by holding the fabric to a light source or using a light box and tracing over the lines. These are shown on the pattern as lines of dashes and 'v's.

Assemble the fabric for the major design into the hoop. Ensure that the fabric is extremely taut and the hoop nut is done up very tightly.

Transfer the design from Tracing Guide 3 onto the second piece of fabric, marking the lines of dashes to be embroidered from the front onto the front of the fabric. Put this piece to one side for now.

Embroidering the major design

Follow the Stitch and Colour Guides in conjunction with the Symbols Chart. Each symbol is numbered, but not necessarily in order of embroidering. Written instructions follow for each number.

1   This is the large sea-green feathery sea fan. The centre line is marked onto the front of the fabric and the sea fan is embroidered from the front, with the loops being made on the back of the fabric. Thread one strand of 1204 in the small punchneedle set at No 3 and embroider with closed feather stitch (see Special Effects, sample b, p52). Vary the length of the outward stitches between 3–5 mm (⅛–³⁄₁₆ in)

2   This is the burnt orange gorgonian coral. Thread six strands of 407 in the medium punchneedle set at No 1 and follow the markings on the pattern.

3   Set the small punchneedle at No 1. Use three strands of 407 and from the front of

Stitch and colour guide 1

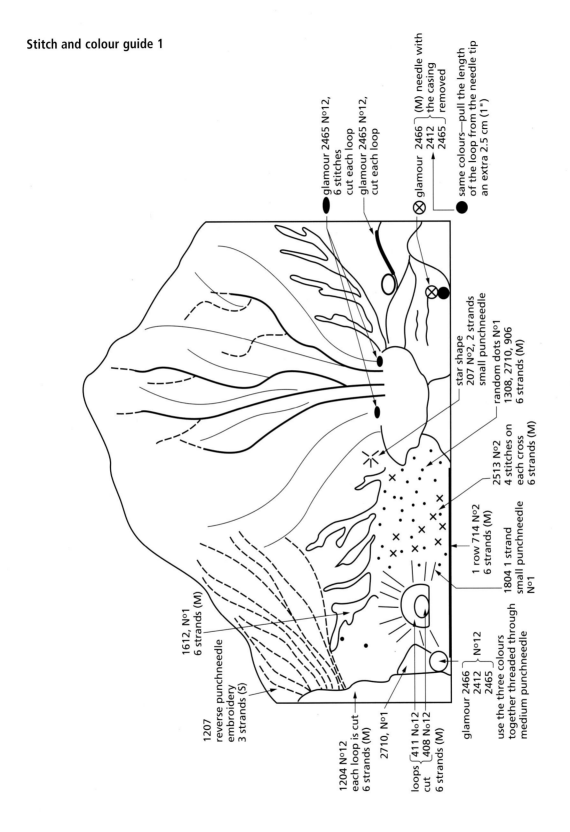

glamour 2465 Nº12,
6 stitches
cut each loop

glamour 2465 Nº12,
cut each loop

glamour 2466 ⎱ (M) needle with
2412 ⎰ the casing
2465 removed

same colours—pull the length
of the loop from the needle tip
an extra 2.5 cm (1")

star shape
207 Nº2, 2 strands
small punchneedle

random dots Nº1
1308, 2710, 906
6 strands (M)

2513 Nº2
4 stitches on
each cross
6 strands (M)

1 row 714 Nº2
6 strands (M)

1804 1 strand
small punchneedle
Nº1

glamour 2466 ⎱
2412 ⎰ Nº12
2465

use the three colours
together threaded through
medium punchneedle

loops ⎱ 411 Nº12
cut ⎰ 408 Nº12
6 strands (M)

2710, Nº1

1204 Nº12
each loop is cut
6 strands (M)

1612, Nº1
6 strands (M)

1207
reverse punchneedle
embroidery
3 strands (S)

Stitch and colour guide 2

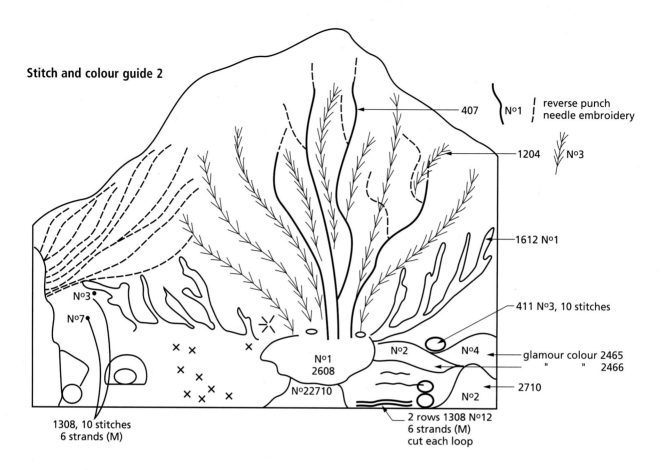

407 · N°1 | reverse punch
needle embroidery

1204 · N°3

1612 N°1

411 N°3, 10 stitches

glamour colour 2465
 "   "   2466

2710

N°2

2 rows 1308 N°12
6 strands (M)
cut each loop

1308, 10 stitches
6 strands (M)

N°3
N°7

N°1
2608

N°22710

N°2   N°4

the piece work reverse punchneedle embroidery (see Stitch Glossary, Figure 3).

4   This is the orange coral. Set the small punchneedle at No 1, threaded with three strands of 207, and from the front of the piece work reverse punchneedle embroidery following the marked lines on the pattern.

5   Use six strands of burgundy 2608 in the medium needle. Set the punchneedle at No 1 and fill in the area.

6   There are four purple areas to fill in following this striped symbol. Use six strands of 2710 in the medium punchneedle and fill in each area either at No 1 or 2 as indicated on the pattern.

7   Rope sponge. Set the punchneedle at No 1. With six strands of 1612 in the medium needle, work the areas shown on the pattern for the sponge.

8   Hot pink mushroom coral. Set the medium

punchneedle at No 12. With six strands of 411 fill in this area, then cut each loop open to give a plush velvet appearance to the coral.

9   Thread the three metallic colours, turquoise, sea green and purple, together through the medium punchneedle set at No 12. Stitch along the two wavy lines shown on the pattern.

10   Use the three colours as in No 9. Set the medium punchneedle at No 12 and work 6 stitches in a circle.

11   Use the three colours as in No 9. Remove the casing from the medium punchneedle and store it and the spring carefully. Work 6 stitches in a circle, ensuring that the needle tip is punched through the fabric up to the blue hilt of the needle. This will make a very long loop on the front of the embroidery.

12   Feather star. These loops are made extra

Symbols chart

0	Symbol	Colour	Strands	Needle size	Needle length	Stitches	
1	 ≪≪≪	1204	1	S	3		mark only the centre line on front of fabric
2	 ∫	407	6	M	1		mark on front of fabric
3	 ⋯	407	3	S	1		
4	 –·–	207	3	S	1		
5	 ▨	2608	6	M	1		
6	‖‖‖‖	2710	6	M	1 & 2		
7		1612	6	M	1		
8	 ⌓	411	6	M	12		
9	 ~	2466 2412 2465		M	12		
10	⊕	II		M	12		
11	⊗	II		M	casing removed	in a circle 6	
12	●	II		M	casing removed	3	
13	▬	2465	1	M	12	in a circle 6	
14	 -------	2465	1	M	12		
15	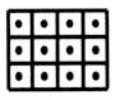 ▦	2465	1	M	4		
16	 ≋ ≋	2466	1	M	2		
17	◉	411	6	M	3	in a circle 10	
18	 OXOXOXOX	1308	6	M	12		
19	 ∿∿∿	714	6	M	2		
20	 ☀	1804	1	S	1		
21	•	1308	6	M	3	in a circle 10	
22	✕	1308	6	M	7	in a circle 10	
23	※	207	2	S	2		
24	 ⫻	1204	6	M	12		
25	✕	2513	6	M	2	in a circle 4	
26	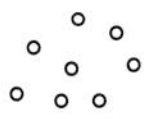 ⁖	1308 906 2710	6	M	1		
27	 ⁙	1791	2	S	with plastic		
28	 ∿	1791	1	S	1		

169

long using the same colours and size of needle as in No 11 above (see Long Loops in Chapter 3 Techniques). To achieve the extra long loops, punch the needle tip to the hilt. Before withdrawing the needle, pull the threads from the eye of needle at the front of the work, thereby extending the loops in length. The longer length allows the loops to fall in the manner of a feather star.

13 Spiny row coral. Set the medium punchneedle at No 12 and with sea green 2465 work 6 stitches in each of the two marked areas. Cut each loop open, which will give a spiky look to the metallic thread.

14 Embroider along this curved line with same colour and needle length as No 13. Cut each loop open.

15 Fill in this area with sea green 2465 and the needle tip set at No 4.

16 Fill in this area with turquoise 2466 and the needle tip set at No 2.

17 Small pink coral. Set the punchneedle at No 3 and with six strands of 411 work 10 stitches in a circle.

18 Set the punchneedle at No 12. With 6 strands of chartreuse 1308 work two rows along the area shown at the base of the pattern.

19 Set the medium punchneedle at No 2. With 6 strands of dark purple 714 work one row along the area shown at the base of the pattern.

20 Take the small punchneedle and set it at No 1. With one strand of pale grey 1804 embroider along the spiky lines surrounding the hot pink mushroom coral (No 8) on the pattern.

21 Set the medium punchneedle at No 3. With six strands of chartreuse 1308 work 10 stitches in a circle.

22 Set the medium punchneedle at No 7. With 6 strands of chartreuse 1308 work 10 stitches in a circle.

23 Set the small punchneedle at No 2. On the front of the embroidery, with two strands of orange 207, embroider a star flower (see Stitch Glossary, Figure 11).

24 The plush sea green area at one side of the pattern. Set the medium punchneedle at No 12. With six strands of sea green 1204 fill in the area. Cut each loop open to give a lovely velvet look.

25 Set the medium punchneedle at No 2. With six strands of musty yellow 2513 work 4 stitches in a circle.

26 The larger dots shown in the lower sections of the pattern are worked at random with three separate colours intermingled throughout—chartreuse 1308, blue 906, purple 2710. Take a look at the photograph to see how this looks.

27 In the areas of finer dots in the upper background of the design, tiny dots are embroidered with the small punchneedle threaded with two strands of Needle Necessities floribunda 1791. Set the needle at No 1 but in this instance a 2 mm (less than ⅛ in) piece of plastic is pushed onto the needle tip to make the length of loop shorter (see Chapter 3 Techniques). Work from the back of the embroidery but 'dance' the needle over the fabric in a similar stitching motion to the meandering stitch (see Stitch Glossary, Figure 9). The tiny dots are not placed too close together, the aim being to fill in all over the background of the embroidery while allowing some colour from the background fabric to show through.

28 This area of meandering stitch is embroidered in meandering stitch on the front of the fabric with one strand of Needle

Necessities floribunda 1791 in the small punchneedle set at No 1.

Finally, from the back of the fabric, using the same colour and needle size as for the tiny dots (27), work a row of loops along the top edge.

Finishing

Trim any long threads on the back.

Remove the fabric from the hoop. Stretch the fabric in all directions to straighten the weave.

Thinly smear You Can Wash It craft glue all over the back of the embroidery. This is to stiffen the fabric so that it will hold its shape when the design is cut out. (Glueing is optional. Many embroiderers are averse to putting glue anywhere near an embroidery.)

It is, however, important to at least glue along the top edge and to ensure that the glue impregnates the fibres of the fabric.

Leave to dry.

With sharp scissors, cleanly cut along the top edge *only*, near the outside of the tiny loops. Sufficient fabric needs to remain on the other three edges for mounting the embroidery into a frame.

Embroidery for the background design

Assemble the fabric for the background design into the hoop. Ensure that the fabric is extremely taut and the hoop nut is done up very tightly.

Orange coral

Set the small punchneedle at No 1, threaded with three strands of orange 207, and from the front of the piece stitch in reverse punchneedle embroidery following the four lines of dashes marked on the pattern.

Soft coral

Embroider the wavy lines indicated with Needle Necessities mayflower 180. Make the loops further apart than usual for a softer appearance.

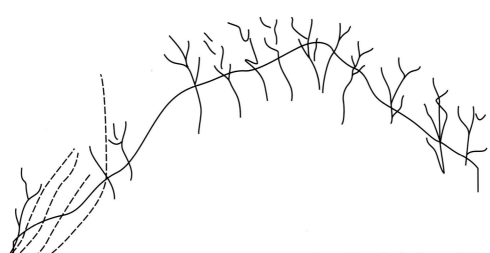

Tracing guide 3 for background design
The line marking the reef is a guide only, used for the final assembly of the embroidery.

Finishing

Place the major embroidery over the minor background embroidery and with a needle and thread, tack the two pieces together at the sides and bottom.

Stitch or glue the seahorse charm into place if you are using one.

Take a little bit of soft cotton wool or wadding (pulled apart) and lightly fill between the two pieces of embroidery to give the illusion of depth. Tuck the filling in so that it cannot be seen.

Frame this colourful embroidery with the shiny feather star cascading over the bottom edge of the chosen matt board.

DELIGHTFUL DOILY

A crisply starched, beautifully embroidered doily evokes memories of yesteryear. Three strands of cotton in lovely pink tones makes this pretty design a joy to embroider.

A NOTE ON OLD FABRICS

I meet many embroiderers who say that they have old, unfinished doilies stashed at home, possibly collected from their forebears. There are a couple of thing to consider with old doilies. One is that the fabric may have deteriorated with age. Secondly, many of the very old doilies are made from linen, and quite often natural fibres such as linen do not take kindly to being 'punched' through. The needle tip can cut the fibres, causing holes to appear. Small holes lead to fraying and loops being unable to stay in place, thus it can happen that, having done a great deal of embroidery, the work may not be able to be completed.

It is best to test the suitability of the fabric of an old doily for punchneedle embroidery. Stitch a 15 cm (4 in) wide border (of any fabric) to two edges to make one corner of the linen doily larger.

This gives added fabric on which to place and tighten the hoop on the outside edge of the fabric so that the test, of just a few stitches, can be made close to the edge of the doily. Refrain from punching into the body of the doily where serious damage to the fabric might occur. Punch some loops close together and then remove them. Check carefully if there has been any damage made to the fibres. If any fibres have been broken and the fabric appears likely to fray, gently undo the work and abandon the idea of using that particular old piece.

Tracing guide

Enlarge at 110%

Colour guide

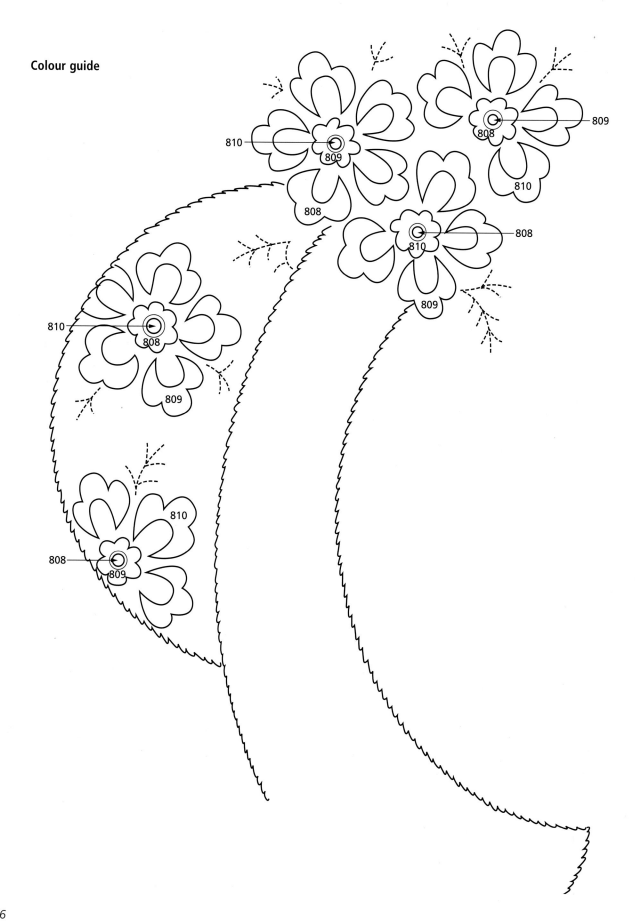

Materials

small punchneedle

2 mm (a little less than ⅛ in) piece of plastic tube

20 cm (8 in) and 25 cm (10 in) lip-lock hoops

pre-printed doily from The Stitchery (see suppliers)
    OR polyester/viscose/flax mix fabric on which
    to trace the design

two fabric doughnuts

iron-on transfer pen

water-erasable pen

sharp embroidery scissors

Threads

	Madeira	DMC
pale pink	808	778
mid pink	809	316
dark pink	810	315
green	1513	522

Preparation

A purchased pre-printed doily will have the design printed on the right side of the fabric. As punchneedle embroidery is worked from the back, the design will need to be traced onto the back of the fabric. It may be that the printed design can be seen from the back, which makes it easy to trace over. If not, however, hold the doily up to a light source so that the design shows through and can be drawn over lightly. Place the fabric in the hoop with the traced design uppermost.

Embroidery

TIP

The use of reverse punchneedle embroidery (see Stitch Glossary, Figure 3) for a domestic piece such as a doily needs to be considered. It is my preference for a piece such as this to work the stems in traditional hand stem stitch embroidery for no other reason than the ease of laundering. With the technique of punchneedle embroidery, where stitches have been embroidered closely together they are very durable and highly washable. It is only where one row of stitching has been worked that due care need to be exercised. Take a note of the photograph, where you will see that the right side of the doily has been completely embroidered with a punchneedle. On the left half, the green stitching for the lines and stems has been hand-embroidered with stem stitch.

It needs to be considered that punchneedle embroidery, which is raised embroidery, may not be ideal for a piece of work on which drinking glasses or such are likely be set down, as the unevenness of the surface may cause a glass to topple. Punchneedle embroidery is, however, wonderful for decorator items, taking the technique into a whole different realm. Even there, one row of reverse punchneedle embroidery is not secure and can possibly be pulled undone if due care is not taken. Therefore, think about the option of using a light smear of glue on the loops which are formed on the back.

For this project, consider using the traditional method of hand sewing with a needle and thread in stem stitch for the lines shown as reverse punchneedle embroidery.

Flower petals

The flower petals are embroidered with the various colours indicated on the colour guide.

Set the punchneedle at No 1 and place the 2 mm piece of plastic (see Short Loops in Chapter 3 Techniques) on the needle and push it up to the handle. Use the needle at this length for all the flower petals.

Flower centres

Work 10 stitches in a circle (see Stitch Glossary, Figure 5) for each flower centre, using the colours shown on the colour guide.

Change to the colour indicated on the colour guide to fill in the remaining area of the centre.

Stems

The stems are worked with reverse punchneedle embroidery (see Special Effects, sample a, p52). When using this method remember to pull the start and

finish threads through to the back and then trim them. Follow the markings on the pattern. Work similarly to feather stitch by starting at the tip and making four stitches, and then work out to the left and back into the centre, working directly over the stitches previously made. Work out to the right and back to the centre. Continue in this manner.

Long curved lines

The curved lines of the pattern are worked last of all with the punchneedle set at No 1, with green 1513, in backwards reverse punchneedle embroidery (see Special Effects, sample h, p54) on the front. Pull the start and finish threads through to the back and then trim them.

The hoop will need to be moved before embroidering the long lines if these are worked in punchneedle embroidery, as not all of the stitching will fit into the hoop. Place a doughnut (see Chapter 3 Techniques) on both the front and back of the doily for protection of the

embroidery as it will be necessary to tighten the hoop over the already completed embroidery.

Assemble the printed fabric with one of the fabric doughnuts on the top and the other underneath. Place the three layers into the hoop and take great care to ensure that the fabric is extremely taut in the hoop. The fabric doughnut does make getting the fabric taut a little more difficult.

Alternatively, complete the embroidery with hand stitching.

Finishing

Remove the fabric from the hoop.

Stretch the fabric in all directions to straighten the weave.

Press carefully by placing the embroidery upside down over a thick, fluffy towel. It is fine to press over the embroidery from the back.

Finish the edge in any manner of your choosing. If the doily is hemstitched, cut away the excess fabric and work a crochet edge.

GRANDMA'S SPECIAL HEART

A pretty heart filled with hearts and kisses to cheer any grandmother. The bright colours and many textures showcase the simplicity and elegance of punch needle embroidery using readily available 6-stranded cottons.

Materials

medium punch needle
20 cm (8 in) lip-lock hoop
30 cm (12 in) square of fabric
iron-on transfer pen
water-erasable pen
sharp embroidery scissors
fine crochet hook
extra fabric to make into a heart-shaped cushion
soft cushion filling
braid maker (optional)

Threads

	Madeira	DMC
lime green	1308	704
darker green	1502	470
dark pink	703	3804
mid pink	701	603
pink	708	3607
light pink	710	3609
white	403	blanc
dark purple	712	553
mauve	802	210
blue	906	793
pale blue	907	794
yellow	109	726
black	2400	310

gold metallic 5017 (optional for the braid) or any gold-coloured thread

Tracing guide

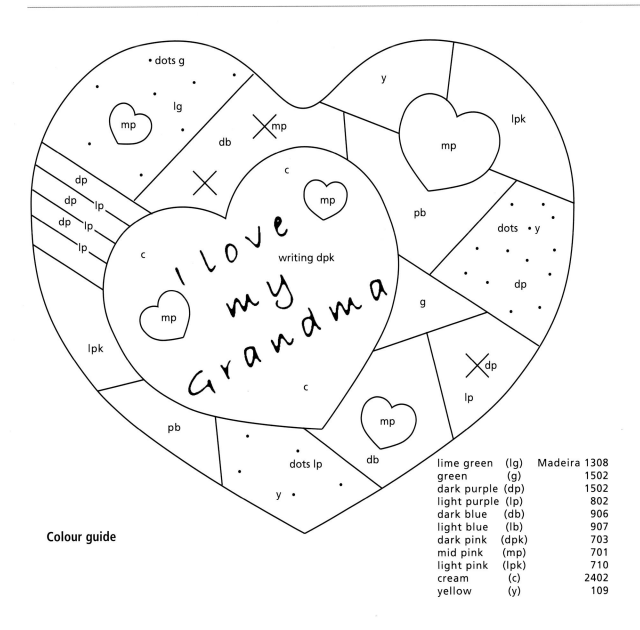

Colour guide

lime green	(lg)	Madeira 1308
green	(g)	1502
dark purple	(dp)	1502
light purple	(lp)	802
dark blue	(db)	906
light blue	(lb)	907
dark pink	(dpk)	703
mid pink	(mp)	701
light pink	(lpk)	710
cream	(c)	2402
yellow	(y)	109

Preparation

Trace the design onto the back of the fabric.

Place the fabric in the hoop with the traced design uppermost, ensuring that the fabric is extremely tight.

Embroidery

Six strands are used throughout in the medium punch needle.

Inner white heart

Set the punch needle at No 1.

Embroider the pink lettering first, with the stitches worked close together.

Work with white around the lettering, ensuring that a space is left between the pink and white stitching. Keep checking the front of the embroidery to see that the stitches are sitting correctly and that the white and pink loops are not entangled with each other. Frequently turn the work to the front, as it may be necessary to move and re-arrange some white loops to allow the pink writing to keep its shape. Use the tip of the small needle to help with this. It might be that a loop here and there will need to be removed or others added to allow the writing to remain readable.

Main heart

Set the punch needle at No 1.

Work one section at a time, following the colours shown on the Colour Guide.

In the light green section at the top of the heart, and in the yellow section at the bottom, dots are marked on the pattern. These are worked as circles. Using the colours indicated on the Colour Guide, make the circles by working 10 stitches in a circle (Stitch Glossary, Figure 5). Embroider the surrounding colour around the dots.

The dark purple section has yellow dots scattered randomly. (To work embroidery for dots see Stitch Glossary, Figure 14.)

As each section is completed, outline it in mid pink using backwards reverse punch needle embroidery (Stitch Glossary, sample h).

Pink heart 1

Commence on the outside edge. Using mid pink, set the punch needle at No 1 and work all the way around the heart. Change the setting to No 2 for the next round and continue changing the length of the needle tip for each following round, up to No 7.

Pink raised velvet heart 2

Start at the outside edge. Using mid pink, set the punch needle at No 3 and work all the way around. Cut each loop on the front. Work another row with the needle set at No 3. Cut the loops.

Work a row at No 4 and cut. Fill in the remaining area at No 5 and cut all the loops. On the front trim and tidy the cut threads.

Pink hearts 3, 4 and 5

These hearts are worked in mid pink, with the needle set at No 1.

Finishing

Trim the threads on the back.

Check that there are no loops standing higher than others on the front. If there are, pull them through to the back with the crochet hook.

Remove the fabric from the hoop and stretch into shape.

Make a black cord, using the cord maker or by hand (see Stitch Glossary) from six 150 cm (60 in) lengths of black thread.

Make two multi-coloured cords by the same technique. For each one, take a 150 cm (60 in) length of each of the dark pink, mid pink, pale blue, darker green and yellow threads which were used in the embroidery, plus a length of gold.

Stitch the black cord and one coloured cord into place on the fabric surrounding the heart before cutting the heart out. If you like, you can shape the coloured cord into a loop at the top of the heart.

Cut out the heart, leaving a 12 mm (½ in) seam allowance all round.

Cut a second heart shape the same as above.

Assembly

Stitch the two heart shapes together to form a small heart-shaped cushion. Leave a small gap and gently fill the cushion with soft wadding. Complete the stitching.

Stitch the second multi-coloured cord into place.

This delightful heart cushion can then be given with love.

SUPPLIERS

Other publications by Pamela Gurney

Punchneedle Embroidery (1997), 5 Mile Press (out of print)

Punch Crazy (1999), Aussie Publishers (out of print)

Punchneedle Embroidery: Dancing Needles (2003), Sally Milner Publishing Pty Ltd

Video *Punchneedle Embroidery*

For the video, available in NTSC and VHS, contact Pamela Gurney at Dancing Needle Designs (see below).

Embroidery supplies

Products by Cameo, Inc
Suppliers of punchneedles and acrylic yarn
2573-DN Forsyth Road
Orlando FL 32807 USA
tel: +1 407 677 1139
fax: +1 407 671 7089

Chandler's Cottage
Suppliers of bag patterns
web: www.chandlerscottage.com

Craftsmart
Suppliers of You Can Wash It and On'N'Off craft glues
4/29 Business Park Drive
Nottinghill VIC 3168 Australia

Dancing Needle Designs
Supplier of all supplies necessary for punchneedle embroidery: punchneedles, books, threads, ribbons, fabric, terracotta pots, pattern packs and kits, cord maker
PO Box 302
Kangaroo Ground VIC 3097 Australia
fax: +61 3 9712 0438
email: pamela@dancingneedles.com or punchemb@bigpond.net.au
web: www.punchneedleembroidery.com and www.dancingneedles.com

DMC
Suppliers of cotton embroidery thread
Australian distributor of DMC:
J Leutenegger Pty Ltd
51-57 Carrington Rd
Marrickville NSW 2204 Australia
web: www.dmc.com

Kakoonda
Suppliers of hand-dyed silk ribbons
PO Box 4073
Langwarrin VIC 3910 Australia

Madeira Threads
Suppliers of cotton embroidery thread
SSS Pty Ltd
16 Valediction Road
Kings Park NSW 2148 Australia
tel: +61 2 9672 3888

Madeira Threads USA (headquarters)
30 Bayside Court (PO Box 6068)
Laconia NH 03246 USA
800 225 3001
tel: +1 603 528 2944
fax: +1 603 528 4264
email: Madeirausa@aol.com

Necessity Notions
Suppliers of overdyed six stranded embroidery cotton
Ben Britim Distributors Pty Ltd
'Vailima'
Scarlett Street
Mittagong NSW 2575 Australia
www.needlenecessities.com

Rajmahal Threads Australia
Suppliers of art silks
182 High Street
Kangaroo Flat VIC 3555
Tel: +61 3 5447 7699
Fax: +1 61 3 5447 7899
email: rajinfo@ozemail.com.au
web: http://www.rajmahal.com.au

The Stitchery
Suppliers of pre-printed doilies and other table linen
59 Cedarwood Drive
Cherrybrook NSW 2126
tel: +61 2 9875 2264